PENGUIN BOOKS
# JOURNEY TO THE EDGE OF THE EARTH

**Joeanna Rebello Fernandes** has worked for over a decade as a features writer with *The Sunday Times of India*, across Mumbai, Chennai and Delhi. She is the author of the children's book *Treasure at the Train Station: An Adventure in Mumbai* (2018), a fantasy set in Victoria Terminus. A freelance writer and editor, she was an editor with Goodearth Publications and was involved in commissioning and editing children's books. She has a master's in English literature and a bachelor's in mass media from the University of Mumbai.

**Cdr Abhilash Tomy KC, NM** is a retired officer of the Indian Navy. He was the first Indian to complete a solo, non-stop circumnavigation of the world under sail in 2013. Cdr Abhilash Tomy also competed in the 2018 Golden Globe Race. He is decorated with the Kirti Chakra, the Nau Sena Medal, the Tenzing Norgay National Adventure Award and the MacGregor Medal for military reconnaissance. He is the recipient of an honorary doctorate.

# Journey to the Edge of the Earth

« A TRUE ADVENTURE »

Joeanna Rebello Fernandes *and*
Cdr Abhilash Tomy, KC, NM (Retd)

PENGUIN BOOKS

An imprint of Penguin Random House

PENGUIN BOOKS

USA | Canada | UK | Ireland | Australia
New Zealand | India | South Africa | China

Penguin Books is part of the Penguin Random House group of companies
whose addresses can be found at global.penguinrandomhouse.com

Published by Penguin Random House India Pvt. Ltd
4th Floor, Capital Tower 1, MG Road,
Gurugram 122 002, Haryana, India

First published in Penguin Books by Penguin Random House India 2022

Text copyright © Joeanna Rebello Fernandes 2022
Story copyright © Commander Abhilash Tomy 2022
Illustrations copyright © Missy Dunaway 2022

ISBN 9780143450139

Typeset in Sabon LT Std by Manipal Technologies Limited, Manipal
Printed at Aarvee Promotions, India

www.penguin.co.in

*For Sandeep, the wind in my sails.*

*—Joeanna*

~~~

*For Vedaant and Abhraneil, and to all the children who wish to sail someday.*

*—Abhilash*

# Contents

# Prologue:
# A Hurricane Arrives

The Indian Ocean is seething. Its waters, blue and well-behaved only hours ago, have now turned dark and dangerous. They snap and snarl and throw up waves like teeth, white and jagged. *Mhadei* and I are in the mouth of a storm.

We rise and fall on the back of the waves, one minute down a watery valley, the next, up a watery cliff. What we see around us changes too, sea—sky, sky—sea. Until it's all sky. Black and swarming, like it's crowded with crows. That's when I realize why it's only the sky I see.

A tremendous wave has reared up under us, carrying *Mhadei* on its shoulders. Higher and higher it climbs, the boat balancing precariously on its knife-edge crest. But not for long. Within seconds, the wave teeters. It topples. We plunge.

*Mhadei* crashes down with a shuddering splash, her prow vanishing under water. She's being swallowed by the sea. The rest of the boat follows the prow down this grey gullet and I go with it. *It's the end*, I think.

But in three short breaths, the boat resurfaces, leaping out of the water like a seahorse. *It's not the end*, I think, but I can't be sure of it.

From the tiny porthole inside the cabin, I size up the hurricane. It's whipping up the waters with a savagery I've never seen before, and I worry my little boat will break from the blows. I can no longer tell where the ocean ends and the sky begins. It looks like crows all over.

Though it's the last thing I want to do in weather like this, I force myself out of the cabin and, through driving sheets of rain, stagger towards the mast. I must check the sails. What would have taken a few quick seconds in less murderous weather now takes long grating minutes, for the boat is pitching violently. Finally, I reach the mast and grab hold of it to steady myself.

And then it comes.

A wave tall as a two-storey building surges slowly out of the ocean, gathering water like a mountain gathers minerals. My back is turned to it, so I don't see its iron fist high above me . . . until it lands squarely on my head. *WHAM!*

I gasp for air as the water sweeps over my face in a flood. Then in a flurry of blows, wave upon wave rains down on me. *Crash, crash, crash.* Overhead, hot wires of electricity splinter the sky and from the cracks comes the drumroll of thunder, loud enough to jolt every sea creature from its deepest sleep. I can't tell the rain apart from the waves, for above or below, the water stings equally.

I lurch back into the cabin, fasten the door to keep it from flooding and strap myself into my bunk. Outside, the ocean continues to bubble and boil like a cauldron over a blazing fire. By now, my hope has fully jumped ship and I am deeply and depressingly convinced that *Mhadei* and I, far from rounding the world, will sooner sink to our graves.

# Boat upon Boat upon Boat

It was the kind of night a boy my age should have been in bed. With a *Phantom* comic and a glass of warm milk. It turned out to be the very opposite of that kind of night.

There I was instead, lacing my patent leather shoes and preparing to go out to what I knew would be a blindingly boring party. Not that I had anything against parties, it was only the kind my parents were invited to that gave me splitting headaches. It was all very well for *them* to say: 'Go play with the other children!' I looked and I looked, but never once spotted children at those parties! Of course, you can't count the ones sleeping on their parents' laps or on the dangerous beds their parents cobbled together by joining two chairs.

'I'm old enough to stay home alone!' I grumbled at my upside-down mother in her downside-up silk sari. Bent double, I glared at her from between my legs as I knotted my second shoe. 'When you're eleven, not seven . . .' she rapped in Malayalam, scotching my next argument with a sticky look.

And so it was that I was led unhappily down the darkening streets of Cochin (now Kochi), my hands trapped in the hands of my parents. They were worried I would bolt back home. And I would too, had I known the way. But the street lights were dim and I couldn't tell where I was. The only thing I could do was show them I was angry. This I did by dragging my feet and kicking up small storms of dust—which my mother hated.

So I dragged harder.

A fishy breeze blew in from the water as if the sea had just burped after a huge seafood dinner. I thought of the buffet table at the party. *I wonder if they'll serve squid.* I loved squid, especially when it was cut into rubbery rings and fried! They were like onion rings from the sea. I loved onion rings too.

Now that I had started thinking about food, I couldn't think of anything else. There might be prawn puffs, mini idlis, chicken sandwiches or fried bananas . . . All of a sudden, I couldn't get there soon enough. *We have to reach before dinner is served and everyone eats up all the squid*, I thought with alarm. I was so worried I started to run, pulling my parents behind me.

'Where are you running?' my father shouted. 'You're going the wrong way!'

~~~

The party was at the Naval Sailing Club, which sat on the edge of an island, one of the dozens that formed the city of Cochin. Bridges connected one island to the next, and if they didn't, you could always travel on a canoe or a ferry.

## The Port City of Kochi

Cocym, Cochym, Ko-Chih, Cochi, Cochin, Kochi—all names lead to the same city. It was ironically a flood that turned Kochi into a world-famous port! When the river Periyar spilled its waters in 1341, it wiped out Muziris, a thriving trade centre on the Malabar Coast. The story goes that this drove merchants and sailors to Kochi, the new natural harbour created by the shape-shifting floodwaters. Kochi now became a thriving port.

Years later, the Portuguese established their first Indian outpost in Kochi, making it the first European fort in India. The city was later settled by the Dutch, and then the British until Independence. Today, it is the headquarters of the Southern Naval Command of the Indian Navy.

My mother told me the maze of water that criss-crossed Kochi's islands was called the backwaters. It was quiet and good-tempered, not like the 'front waters'—a name I came up with for the Arabian Sea that beat the beaches of our hometown without ever stopping. Never.

By the time we arrived at the sailing club, it was noisy like the front waters. Wave after wave of jangling music poured from the windows and fell upon us. The party seemed to be well underway.

My father served in the Indian Navy. When you're in the navy, your office is usually on the water or near it. The officers made new friends wherever they went. There were always parties to welcome them and—in the time it took for new friends to become fast friends—parties to say goodbye to them.

This time, goodbyes were being said to a man called Krishnamurthy, who had been posted to Visakhapatnam, the headquarters of the Indian Navy on the east coast of the country. Everyone gathered around him, saying nice things about how they wished he wasn't leaving and how much they'd miss him.

My parents were soon sucked into the whirlpool, and I was left to my own devices. *What to do? What to do?* I wondered. The buffet table was bare as an Indian beach in July. It meant dinner hadn't yet been served, which meant the squid was safe.

'Excuse me . . .' I said, pulling at a waiter's white waistcoat, 'when will dinner be served?'

'Not for another hour,' the man said, smiling.

Enough time to allow me to explore the club grounds. 'Can I go outside?' I asked my mother. My father answered instead, 'As long as you stay close to the building and don't fall into the water.'

I don't think anyone would *choose* to fall anywhere, much less into the dark backwaters, but I locked that thought behind my teeth.

On my way out the door, I caught sight of a pile of snacks on a table and, quietly wrapping four prawn cutlets in a paper napkin, slipped the package into my pocket. There was an enormous fish tank in the lobby. I padded up to it and pressed my nose to the glass. Fat catfish swam lazily in the tube-lit water. Their thick lips and scanty whiskers reminded me of my friend's father. I chuckled, imagining Uncle Mathew swimming in the tank.

He'd make a good fish, I decided.

Tired of this, I walked out to the front porch of the club. A path led from there to the back of the building, where it was swallowed whole by thick black shadows. 'Follow me,' the path said. So I did. The long tongues of the coconut palms along the garden's edge soughed *tssh tssh tssh*. But I didn't stop to listen.

Suddenly, I spied something ahead of me. Dark and glinting, it shifted slightly where it stood. My toes curled and my ears furled. I was just about to barrel back to the clubhouse, when . . . with a heave of relief, I realized what it was—the backwaters. It lay there, still as a serpent, with tiny waves gleaming like scales in the moonlight.

If the waters were here, so were the Chinese fishing nets. I raced to the slipway, the ramp leading down to the water's edge, to spot them. Cochin was full of these nets, lined up along the banks like upturned handkerchiefs, as if waiting to catch something from the sky instead of the sea.

But just as I reached the ramp, my eyes snapped to the left. Under a shed made up of nothing but a roof and a couple of columns, a bank of bright yellow lights beamed down on broad wooden racks, mounted one above the other like bookshelves. And on those racks sat something I would never forget my whole life. BOATS!

Rows upon rows of stunning dinghies, kayaks and canoes were stacked neatly, four boats high, each to its own rack. They looked

like enormous roosting birds. The light bouncing off their gleaming hulls stretched lean and long—red and yellow, blue and green, white and orange.

My mouth fell open in astonishment, still cupping a piece of a half-eaten cutlet. I had, of course, seen boats before. But those were either waist-deep in water or flipped over on the beach to dry like washed bowls. These boats, however, were entirely different. They were neither on sand nor on water, but high up in the air.

*Perhaps they're special*, I thought excitedly. *Perhaps they're not made for the sea at all, but for the sky! Perhaps they fly! Is that why they're all stacked up like this?*

I decided to climb into one to see if this was true. My mind started to swim with scenes of how it would play out . . . *There would be a button or a switch, of course. And when it was turned on, the boat will judder a little, lift a few inches into the air, move slowly out of its slot . . . and then whizz away . . . I could probably even steer it with my mind!*

My hands and legs scrambled to catch up with my thoughts. I grabbed hold of the metal post, placed one foot on the lowest rack, and was about to hoist myself up on to the platform when I heard a throat clear itself in the shadows.

*Ahem, ahem.*

My heart exploded like a pricked balloon, and in terror, I tumbled to the ground. A large shape bent over me, and out of it separated a smaller shape. A hand. It fastened itself to my arm, and with a firm but not unkind tug, pulled me upright.

'And where were you about to sail off to, little man?'

# Where Is the Sea of Tranquillity?

I looked up into the face that spoke and was relieved to find it wasn't a ghost, or a pirate or worse, one of my father's friends. It was a spectacled man with skin that gleamed as though, just like the hulls of the boats behind me, he too had been vigorously varnished. His hair was grey, but his neat moustache was shockingly black. This amazed me. I did not know a person's hair could be two different colours. *Do different parts of the body grow old at different speeds?* I asked myself, marvelling at the idea.

Or maybe I said it out loud, because the man grunted, 'What?'

'Oh, sorry, uncle,' I replied in a hurry, 'I only wanted to see if these boats could fly.'

'Fly!' the man repeated, his face scrunching up in suspicion. Then a laugh exploded from his moustached mouth. Not meanly, but as if he had had the same idea himself.

'You know, I've *seen* boats fly,' he said in a low, shrouded voice. Then, straightening up, he pointed to an old wooden bench nearby. 'Come, sit. Are you with the party?'

'Yes,' I said. We sat on the bench, side by side.

'You know, I've spent my whole life with boats, and I can tell you, they're the bravest, the most heroic of all things that move on Earth.

Not even an aeroplane can do the sort of things a boat can,' he said stoutly. 'My name is Paul, by the way. What's yours?'

'Abhilash,' I said, looking up at Paul, puzzled. 'But how can a boat be brave?' I looked at his spectacles. They were so thick that Paul's eyes were apple seeds behind them.

'I can tell you stories about tiny boats—no larger than this bench here—that have sailed for days and days on the ocean with nothing but a sail to pull them along. No motor, nothing. Have you ever seen the ocean?' he turned to ask me.

'I've seen the sea. But I've never swum in it,' I said truthfully, although I had told my friends I'd swum right up to the horizon.

'How do you know where the sea ends and the ocean begins?' I asked Paul. 'Also, how do you know where one ocean ends and another begins?' It was a question that had troubled me ever since my father brought home the table globe. At first, I thought the lines that criss-crossed the globe also divided the oceans into neat little compartments. But then I saw it wasn't true. All the oceans on the globe—the Indian, Atlantic, Pacific and Arctic (and later, what came to be called the Southern Ocean)—spilled right across those lines. Lats and longs they were called, I recalled.

'Those are very good questions,' Paul said approvingly. 'To answer the first one, seas are waterbodies close to land. They're sometimes surrounded by it on all sides, like the Caspian Sea. *That*, in fact, is a very large lake. And sometimes, a sea is only surrounded by land on some sides, like the Arabian Sea, which is somewhere over there,' he said, pointing to the right. 'Can you name a sea no one has nor can ever sail?'

'The Dead Sea?' I ventured a guess.

'Don't be sea-lly... Get it?' he guffawed, appreciating his own joke. 'It's the Sea of Tranquillity. And do you know where that is?'

He pointed up. 'On the moon! It's not really a sea, you see, just a large bowl of moon dust!'

I looked up at the moon. No one had ever told me there were a sea there, real or imaginary.

'Now for your second question,' he continued, more seriously, 'I don't think you can *or should* divide the oceans into parts. It's bad enough that people slice up land, saying this belongs to your country and this belongs to mine. If humans found a way to live on water, I'm sure they'd divide that too into countries and states. Can you imagine building walls and fences on the ocean!' He grinned, even though his brow was bunched with worry lines. 'If you really want to know, all the world's oceans are just one gigantic ocean. They're only named after their basins . . . you know, the floor or ground underneath them. For example, the Pacific Ocean should rightly be called the Pacific Basin. Do you understand?'

'Yes,' I said, but my mind whispered, 'No.'

A cool wind rose off the water and quietly blew into our faces.

'The ocean, you know,' continued Paul, carving a wide arc in the air, 'is like the sky. Infinite. It does not end. Or at least it feels that way when you're on it. It covers nearly the whole Earth, leaving only a quarter to land. Imagine if there was only a single star in the sky,' he suddenly said, pointing up. 'That's a boat in the middle of the ocean. Now wouldn't you call that a brave boat?'

I looked up, trying to imagine a single boat in that black sea of a sky.

*I'd like to be that boat*, I thought.

It turned out, Paul knew a lot about oceans because he was a sailmaker. Those white triangles I drew on paper boats, Paul made them from canvas and fixed them to real boats! The only people I had ever imagined around a boat were sailors and pirates, and of course, fishers and ferry-folk. Not a man with wood and a hammer, or cloth and a needle!

'Sewing sails isn't like sewing a pair of pants, you know,' Paul pointed out. 'It's a science. Boats come in different shapes and sizes, each requiring its own special sail. And what is a sail? The cup that catches the wind that moves the boat! A bad sail is like a cracked cup. It can scatter the wind and topple the boat, you know.'

I realized Paul was greatly interested in facts and knowledge. He also said 'you know' a lot, which probably meant he wanted me to know things too.

'But, Paul,' I began. 'You said you'd seen boats fly. Are you taking me for a ride?' It was a line I had learnt from my cousin.

'What does that mean?' he asked, puzzled.

'It means, are you making up stories?' I said, pleased to be teaching an adult something for a change.

## Seas of the Moon

Before astronomers knew better, they believed there was an ocean on the moon . . . and seas, and lakes and marshes. They believed this because when they gazed up, they saw dark patches they took for waterbodies. When the telescope was invented in the early seventeenth century, astronomers were able to see the moon up close. They counted all its 'seas' (lunar maria in Latin), giving each 'waterbody' a name such as Sea of Vapours, Sea of Clouds, Sea of Moisture, Bay of Dew, Lake of Sorrow, Lake of Forgetfulness, Marsh of Epidemics, Marsh of Sleep, Ocean of Storms. These names are still around, even though we now know the dark patches are nothing but basaltic lava that flowed over the moon's surface about 3.9 billion years ago, when large celestial bodies crashed into it.

'My friend, I never lie . . . except maybe to the doctor. But of course, I *have* seen boats fly, you know. Not in the way you've seen birds or planes or dragonflies fly. A boat stretches out its long white sails like the wings of an albatross, and when it catches the wind, it lifts clean off the water, hull barely scraping the waves.' His voice had gone soft and feathery, like it was describing a dream. 'You'll see it too one day. And then you'll know what I mean—boats are the birds of the ocean-sky!'

# The Storyteller Sailmaker

Paul's stories about the sea were not just time-travelling, but place-travelling inventions. He had an endless supply of them, and I begged my father to take me back to the club so I could travel far and wide. Dad knew old Paul was filling my head with brine, but he didn't mind.

As soon as we'd reach the club, I'd let go of my father's hand and race around to the back, looking for the old sailmaker. He was almost always inside his little workshop bent over a sail by the window, needles and tacks strewn about his wooden worktable like crumbs on a plate. Strapped around his right hand was a brown leather band called a palm. It protected his hand from the thick needles he used to sew the sails.

'Where to today, captain?' He'd grin as soon as I'd enter the little room.

'The Caribbean Sea,' I'd command, settling on a three-legged stool.

Or

'The Strait of Malacca.'

Or

'The Gulf of Aqaba.'

I'd pluck names of oceans, seas, bays and straits from the world map on my bedroom wall, and every time I'd visit Paul, I'd throw a new name at him. Paul would expertly catch it, throw a line down into his mind and fish out a story, which always began with the question: 'Have you heard of . . .

'. . . the pirate Boysie Singh, who fed his hostages to the Caribbean sharks?'

'...*The Flying Dutchman* that was swallowed by a storm off the Cape of Good Hope? It turned into a ghost ship that is doomed to sail forever with its crew of the dead.'

'...Ching Shih, the Chinese pirate who commanded a fleet of 1800 junks in the South China Sea? Did you know this pirate was a woman?!'

'...the six young men who built a wooden raft called the *Kon Tiki* and sailed with a parrot across the Pacific for 101 days, all the way from Peru to the Polynesian islands?'

I tasted salt on my tongue and felt the wind worming through my ears as I travelled to parts of the world my eyes had never seen and my brain had never known. Every story carried me away—on a brig, a brigantine, a barque, a raft, a sloop, a junk, a canoe—and each time I sailed, I was the captain of the ship.

One day, I was Kunjali Marakkar I, the Muslim sea captain of Calicut, who made the Portuguese wish they had never left Lisbon.

The next day, I was Kanhoji Angre the big-moustached Maratha who snuck up to sack English and Portuguese vessels in the dead of night.

The day after that, I was Leif Erikson the Norse explorer, clipping across the Atlantic on my Viking vessel, to become the first European to land in North America ...

'Paul, you know ...' I once announced after we returned from another watery tale, 'I think I'd like to become a sailor when I grow up.'

Paul was mid-stitch when he paused, and looking at me through the needle's eye, clucked his tongue. 'Captain, I think you're going to be more than that—I think you're going to be an explorer.'

'How do you know?' I asked him, raising an eyebrow.

'How do you not?' he shot back, raising two.

Time flowed like water, and I flowed with it on a paper boat. By now, my family had left Cochin. And like my father's friend, Krishnamurthy, my father too was given a sobbing send-off at the sailing club.

We spent several years moving up and down the west coast of India— from Karanja, a naval station near Bombay (now Mumbai), on to Bombay itself, back down the coast to Aluva in Kerala, until we finally found ourselves once more in Cochin.

Like all children of the navy, I studied at various Kendriya Vidyalaya schools. Every new transfer meant a new campus, new teachers, new classmates. While other children made friends easily, I kept mostly to myself, reading books as though my life depended on it. Maybe it did. I swallowed book after book after book like a whale swallows krill. But of all the stories, I always drifted towards the ones set at sea: *Moby Dick. Treasure Island. Robinson Crusoe. Twenty Thousand Leagues Under the Sea.* Even when I slept, I dreamt of books and the sea.

'What is it?' my mother asked curiously one morning. She had entered my room to pluck me out of bed and found me grinning stupidly at the ceiling.

## The World's Largest Floating Bookstore and Library

Logos Hope is a 12,000-ton passenger ferry that sails from country to country with over 5000 books. The world's largest floating bookstore and library, it has been visited by over eight million people since its launch in February 2009. GBA Ships, the organization that runs it, ran three other ship libraries: Logos, Doulos and Logos II, although today, only the Logos Hope floats. At every port of call, thousands of visitors stream into the ship to browse and buy books they may never find in their local bookshops and libraries. Incidentally, one of the early voyages of GBA's very first floating library, the Logos, was to Cochin in India in 1971!

'I had the best dream of my life, Mummy!' I said, 'I was on a huge ship in the middle of the ocean . . . I don't know where . . . and I was absolutely, totally alone. And all around, in tall towers everywhere, in every cabin and across the decks, were BOOKS! Millions of them. All kinds—comics, mysteries, adventures, encyclopaedias, even dictionaries! I had all the time in the world to read them because there was nothing else to do. The ship just sailed itself around!'

She smiled sweetly down at me. 'That's a lovely dream, son. But,' mouth twisting, she snapped, 'before you sail away on that book-boat of yours, there's another boat waiting for you . . . It's called a "bus"! And you'll find plenty of books where it's taking you. Now get up and get dressed for school!'

# School on the Sea, School in the Sky

All the stories Paul told me, and all the books I'd read bubbled inside my brain during my years in school, and by the time I turned seventeen, a single word swam up from the zillions: 'adventure'. There was only one thing to do—find it.

It was now time to choose a college to prepare for the working life I would have as an adult. But I couldn't see myself cooped up in an office building. I wanted something exciting and dangerous... something that would take me to the verge of a volcano, the pinnacle of a mountain, the gullet of a geyser. I couldn't, *wouldn't* allow my life to pass by like a fast train to Pointless Point.

By then, I had come to the conclusion that the only possible place I would find adventure was the sea or the sky. Both equally exciting. Both equally expansive—that is, roomy enough to let me have my adventure in peace, without being jostled by anyone else. What I could not make up my mind about was whether I ought to go seawards or skywards. But this conundrum was sorted out soon enough when I realized the one organization that controlled a fair bit of the sea *and* sky around India was the same one my father served—the Indian Navy. They had ships *and* planes, and if I was lucky, I might have a good chance at both.

Luck, however, had absolutely nothing to do with it.

To get into the Indian Navy, I had to pass a knuckle-breaking battery of tests. The first of these was a written exam that was attempted by a couple of hundred thousand students from all corners of the country!

Thankfully, after weeks of non-stop studying and dozens of desk-dinners, I sailed through it and proceeded to the next lap of the race, the interview. For this important part of the assessment, I had to board a train and travel to the heart of India, to the city of Bhopal in the state of Madhya Pradesh.

~~~

It was a bone-dry day in March when I stepped off the footboard of the train, exhausted and bedraggled after a juddering two-day journey from Kochi (the city had now changed its name).

Gathering my luggage from under my seat, I flagged down a taxi outside the railway station and drove to the campus of the Service Selection Board of the Indian Navy. This was the department in charge of recruiting naval officers. At the gates of the leafy defence estate, I fell in with a thick stream of young men and some women, who, like me, were nervously making their way to Round Two of the try-outs.

At the basketball court, each of us was given a number bib as large as a billboard.

'These will be your identification badges,' hollered the soldiers who handed them out. 'Wear them across your chest at all times. Except, of course, to bed.'

While the bibs were large enough to keep the food off our shirts, they served a more sinister purpose. Their 10-inch digits helped the naval examiners identify us from even a hundred feet away! Like spies, these officers fanned out across the campus, stealthily noting how we walked and talked outside the exam halls, when we thought no one was watching us. Oh, but they were!

After scrutinizing us for four days—as if through a magnifying glass—the examiners were finally ready with their roll-call of selected candidates. The bunch of us trooped out to the basketball court on jellied feet. This was our make-or-break moment. Those who made the cut would be asked to stay back for Round Three, the medical exams; the rest would have to go crying home. I could hear teeth chattering nervously around me. They could have been my own.

One by one, our numbers were loudly called out and two groups started to form on the court, grinning on one side, groaning on the other.

'*Bacha log iss taraf, sahib log uss taraf* (children here, gentlemen there),' a jawan barked. The ones who made it were already being called sahibs, their fates sealed. I waited anxiously for my own. When it was announced, the single bead of sweat that had started to sprout on my temple promptly evaporated.

With a beam as broad as a brig, I strode over to the side of the sahibs. I was (almost) in the navy!

Only I wasn't.

While the rejected candidates were packing up to leave, the selected ones were limbering up for the stringent medical inspection. Over two eye-watering weeks, we would be put through a string of tests that would chalk the full measure of our bodies—from the stamina of our limbs to the suppleness of our spines.

Now, while I wasn't overly athletic and had about a quarter of the physique of your standard-issue bodybuilder, I thought I was at least *fit enough* to sail through the physical examination. I had misled myself.

I was discovered to have a deviated nasal septum (the wall between my nostrils leaned to one side). *And* I had mild dorsal scoliosis (my spine was also off-kilter by some degrees from the standard). The prognosis? Strenuous work, the doctors believed, would tire me out quickly . . . and life in the navy, as everyone knew, was no picnic. In the end, like the 'bacha log', I too was asked to pack up and go home.

But I wasn't about to give up so easily. Both problems could be set right, I was assured. All I had to do was undergo a minor surgery to fix my nose, and have my back re-examined by a different doctor. 'You're lucky,' the new doctor said. 'The reading just about falls within the navy's permitted range. That's why it's always a good idea to get a second opinion,' he added, charging no fee for this additional advice.

With nose straightened and back levelled, I reapplied for another medical examination. And this time, I made it right past the gates.

~~~

I was still seventeen in the July of '96, when my father, my younger brother Aneesh and I travelled to Goa, guarding a black steel trunk between us. The trunk contained everything I would need for my new life at the Indian Naval Academy. With no direct train from Kochi, we rattled down to Mangalore (now Mangaluru) in the back of a state-run bus, and from there bounced all the way to Panaji (once Panjim), the capital city of Goa, in another rickety bus. By the time we rolled into the terminal, every bone had switched places in my body and I fell in a sore heap at the foot of the battered Maruti Omni taxi that had materialized to take us along on the last leg of our journey.

As we drove down red-mud roads made soupy by monsoon rains, past paddy fields with their neat rows of spiky young rice stalks, I started to feel at home. *This is hardly different from Kochi*, I said to myself, with some relief. I was about to live far from my family for the first time in my life, and though I was excited, I was already homesick. *Anything that looked like home would make me feel at home*, I thought.

But I would soon learn, for all its outward resemblance, the world I was stepping into couldn't be more different from the one I had just left.

This was the world of the INS *Mandovi*, the Naval Academy, a hothouse of reveilles, drills, exercises, six-a-day roll-calls, boots, books and boats. While the rest of Goa basked on their balconies, sipping port and eating bebinca, I was to be squeezed within the academy's thick military walls, between its tight military timetables, until I would emerge, four full and frazzling years later, an Indian Naval officer.

I knew none of that yet.

After they deposited me in my room and took a quick tour of the grounds, my father and brother prepared to leave in the same taxi by which we had arrived. But before getting in, Dad placed a heavy hand on my shoulder and said in a quiet voice, 'Son, today, you go in a boy, but you'll come out a man.' Then he threw his arms around me.

As I watched them drive down the road, my heart turned into a small water balloon, heavy and rolling, threatening to lurch any moment off the ledge of my chest and burst. Later that night, it did.

~~~

The academy was situated in the village of Verem by the river Mandovi. Coconut trees bristled on both riverbanks. As I walked down the roads, I could see cottages through the trees painted purple-pink, fluorescent yellow and bottle green—colours so exotic the houses looked like cake. Overhead, blue kingfishers perched on electricity cables hung low like bunting down the village roads. And through it all flowed the river, so languid it didn't seem to be moving at all, in no hurry to meet the sea.

My days at the academy rushed by in a blur. The subjects were new and exciting: seamanship, maritime history, naval drills, weapons, boat handling, naval communications . . . I learnt everything there was to learn about the soldier's life at sea. At first, these were dry lessons from textbooks, but later we had actual practice on the water itself.

Lessons included, but were not limited to

- reading complicated sailing instruments like the mariner's compass and the sextant (this was before the days of GPS);

- making sense of pilot books and complicated nautical charts with their maze of tiny numbers and shaded patches that looked like abstract art;
- plotting a ship's course on open water, which is something like finding your way in the dark;
- pegging the position of a vessel with nothing but the sun and stars as pointers;
- understanding the motion of ocean currents and the many moods of the wind;
- keeping a meticulous ship log;
- gauging the depth of a seabed by the shape of swells and the colour of waves.

Everything was fascinating to me and I absorbed it all like a sea sponge.

One year blended into the next and I found I didn't mind the long hours and hard work. In fact, I had grown to enjoy my disciplined life at the academy. By Year Three, I even found myself at the centre of the academy's sailing circle as captain of the sail team.

Our boats were the blue-sailed Enterprise, pretty little dinghies built for two. We did not have a sailing coach to train us for competitions at the time, and the stiff task of knocking our team into shape fell to me. But I had no clue what to do! So I turned to the only instructor I knew on campus—the academy library. There, I read every book I could find on sailboat racing rules, sailing manoeuvres, strategy and tactics. And when we put those lessons to practice, to my surprise (and relief), we actually managed to win a few competitions!

Now, books may have taught me how to tack, duck and cross other boats on the sea, but they could offer no useful advice on how to tackle that dreaded monster with a savage appetite for young cadets (naval students) . . . what the French poetically call *mal de mer*, and the rest of us call seasickness! As it turned out, it was not in a little dinghy, but on a sprawling, white-hulled, three-masted barque that I met the slimy beast.

The INS *Tarangini* was the kind of ship eighteenth-century sailors took out for a spin, with its stack of square sails billowing in the breeze like bedsheets hung out to dry. It was on such a ship that we sailed from Goa to Mumbai in our fifth term. Having captained the sail team with some amount of success, I had loftily presumed I was built for all kinds of boats and all varieties of water. But it was only after I felt the steep lurching in my stomach at the start of that fateful run that I knew I had presumed too much. Over three queasy days—the entire length of our passage—I faithfully contributed the insides of my stomach to the sea at various points along the way, until we docked in Mumbai and I was led to land with my nauseous head between my knocking knees.

Thankfully, by the time I had completed my naval training and was commissioned into the Indian Navy on 1 July 2000, I had sprouted a stouter pair of sea legs. From then on, no matter how big the boat or how churlish the sea, I was never again caught insides-out!

*(I learnt later that the word 'nausea', which was originally used to describe seasickness, has its roots in the Greek* naus *for 'ship'. Guess what! The Sanskrit* nau *means 'ship' too. From these roots come a fleet of other related words like navigation, navy, argonaut, astronaut and nautilus.)*

~~~

Our job in the navy was to protect the country from dangers sneaking in—not only *on* the water but *under* and *above* it as well, on submarines and even on planes zipping across the seas. *You joined the navy to sail and fly,* I reminded myself. And now that I'd learnt everything there was to know about ships and submarines, I looked up to the sky.

To learn to fly the navy's planes, I had to train with the Indian Air Force, the aerial wing of the Indian military. So that's where I headed—to the Basic Flying Training School at the Bamrauli airbase in Allahabad, Uttar Pradesh.

On the morning of my first day in the field (I had finished with the textbook lessons by now), I crossed the hot asphalt to what would be my tiny classroom in the clouds: the HAL-HPT 32, an aircraft large enough only for the instructor and me. A million butterflies, like stowaways, crowded my stomach.

The instructor and I took our seats in the cockpit.

'Are you nervous?' he asked with a grin.

*What do you think!* I said in my mind. But out loud, 'Just a little.'

'No need to worry, we'll be up and down in no time,' he said, trying to reassure me, before snapping down the visor of his helmet.

I didn't like the sound of that. 'Up and down' had an ominous ring to it. I pictured an egg, flung up and crashing down.

I looked straight ahead through the windscreen at the airstrip. It stuck out like a long taunting tongue ahead of me.

So I looked up at the sky. It was blue as the sea. Now that was a colour I was familiar with.

The instructor took the controls first to show me how it was done. He taxied slowly down the runway for some distance, and when he had built sufficient momentum, pulled back the throttle and arced up. We curved a smooth wide circle in the air before gliding down and bumping gently back on the runway. It seemed easy enough.

Now it was my turn. I quickly glanced over the bank of switches and dials on the control panel in front of me, and then I too rolled down the runway. After a couple of minutes, I gripped the thrust lever and pulled back. The silver wings of the aircraft gleamed like mercury as the plane lifted off the ground and climbed steeply up the air. As I rose, the butterflies in my stomach swept up and streamed out of my ears. I felt weightless as I pulled away from the planet, watching

gravity's long rope snapping clean. For the first time in my life, I was wholly and utterly free.

The flight was to be one of many. I went on to spend countless elevating hours in the HAL-HPT 32 before I left Allahabad and headed to Bangalore (now Bengaluru) in the southern state of Karnataka, where I learnt to fly a very different breed of bird—the Dornier 228.

This was a larger aircraft that could carry up to nineteen passengers or their equivalent weight in cargo. I spent five months in this new classroom, mastering all the acrobatics it allowed. And when I finally completed the course, I was formally inducted into the Indian Naval Air Arm's fixed-wing division as a reconnaissance pilot! Eyes peeled for trouble, my job was to patrol the sea from the sky. From my cockpit, I could see the earth stretching for miles up to the horizon's finish line, curving slightly at the edges, while all around me clean white clouds piled high like soapsuds in skies clear as water.

Yet it was not the blue up above, but the blue down below to which my heart swivelled, and my bones told me: There, down there, Abhilash, is where your Grand Adventure lies.

## Indian Navies

While ancient and medieval Indian kings kept ships for trade and transport, one of the earliest to set up an admiralty—an office to monitor ports, sailing vessels and sailor-soldiers—was Chandragupta Maurya, in the fourth century BCE. This department, which was part of the kingdom's war office, was headed by an officer called the Navadhyaksha or 'Superintendent of Ships'. Mauryan naval ships protected merchant vessels from pirates and destroyed enemy craft.

Even as most early Indian navies were formed to defend their kingdoms, one empire deployed its navy to attack and conquer other lands. This was the Chola Empire of the south, whose navy stands out in Indian maritime history for its size and might. Right from the tenth century CE, the Cholas used their ships to expand their domain. Their fleet helped them capture Sri Lanka, the Maldives, parts of Indonesia, Malaysia and Thailand, making them the first Indian dynasty to spread their net far beyond India via the sea.

# Cast Off

In the winter of 1911, a king-sized plaster-of-Paris arch rose by the sea at Apollo Bunder (now Wellington Pier) in Bombay. A gigantic doorway to the city, it had been mounted to welcome a supremely important ship to Indian shores: the HMS *Medina*. Within the ship's sumptuous cabins luxuriated none other than the king and queen of England, George V and Mary, who were shortly to be crowned emperor and empress of India! On the afternoon of 2 December, to a raucous reception of hundred-and-one spitting guns and a million-and-one cheers and whistles, the white-clad sailor king stepped through the arch. It was called the Gateway of India.

Exactly 101 years later, on another wintry afternoon, another sailor passed through the arch. A commoner this time. By now, the Gateway of India had been toughened up and set in stone . . . or basalt rock when you looked closer. And the sailor wasn't stepping *on* Indian shores but stepping *off* it, not on an elephantine ocean liner but a tiny 56-foot sailboat, a sloop.

The sloop was a pert little boat, egg white above the waterline and tar black below it, with a cool blue band circling her hull like a belt. From her deck soared a 69-foot mast that was as tall as a seven-storey building, and from the top of this mast, ropes ran down like streamers from a maypole. She was the INSV *Mhadei*. And I was her captain!

Just like King George, I too drew a crowd. It was less than one-thousandth of what *he* had managed over a century ago, but still, it was the grandest goodbye *I* had ever received in my life. And at a public monument no less! The Gateway was dressed up for the day, with a quarter-kilometre-long plum-purple banner draped around its

parapet like a sash. All it needed was a bow, and the only bows within fishing distance were attached to the boats in the harbour. (But those were 'bows' to rhyme with 'hows', not 'bows' to rhyme with 'toes'.)

Below the arch, sailors, policemen and journalists eddied in and out of a canopied enclosure, eating fat samosas and drinking sweet tea despite the sweltering noon heat. I would have liked a coffee myself to straighten my nerves, but someone or other kept pulling me away from the buffet counter. If it wasn't a journalist hustling a last-minute interview, it was a landlubber offering unwanted advice.

'Good luck, young man,' barked a stranger. 'Stick to the middle and try not to drown.'

'Stick to the middle? Of the ocean?' I asked incredulously. Did he think I was sailing down a highway? 'Thanks. I'll try.'

Over a hundred people milled about me, most of whom I had never clapped eyes on before. I was unused to such a fuss and the attention, though flattering, was a little stifling. It was like being hugged by too many sweaty aunts at a Christmas dinner. My eyes kept drifting to my watch. 'Soon . . . soon . . .' I soothed myself.

But there *were* faces in that crowd I *was* happy to see, and these were fixed firmly to my friends. Many had brought me little gifts, like a small figurine of Ganapati, the elephant-headed god of good beginnings, and a rosary, the string of little beads with which Christians pray. I would add the presents to the horde I had already amassed on the boat—a pirate's plunder of apples, pickles, crucifixes and back issues of *National Geographic*.

'Take a book along in case you get bored,' grinned a friend, hiding something behind his back. 'In fact, here, take a couple.' And he thrust a thick stack of *Tinkle* comics at me.

'Thank you, man, I'll add them to my floating library,' I laughed, accepting the magazines gladly. Everyone who knew me well knew I loved nothing better than to read. Crime thrillers, science journals, comics, even books on maths and world history, any book I could lay my hands on. I absorbed print like blotting paper absorbs ink. Even on short sorties with the navy, when sailing from Mumbai to Goa or Kochi to Karanja, as soon as work was done, I'd sprawl out on the deck with a book held above me, a little tent pitched in another world.

Suddenly, a thought struck me. Hadn't it all started with just that—a book? A very very specific book? With a periscope eye, I scanned the crowd for its owner, for it was that book and its reader that set me off on what was to become the journey that would change my life!

I didn't have to look long, for not even a thousand people could swallow the strapping figure of Vice Admiral Manohar Prahlad Awati!

## The Sailor Who Sailed a Country Around the World

If you were to club all the great captains of all the great sea legends into a single person, he would take the storybook shape of the man who stood in front of me now. With a milk-white mariner's cap, a matching moustache that fanned out to meet his beard, and a booming voice that could bring the greatest ships to heel, Admiral Awati was the picture of every hardy sea salt that had ever weighed anchor since the dawn of sailing.

If I owed my imminent adventure to any one person, it was him.

Many years ago, when the vice admiral was a young naval student in England, he read a book that knocked his socks off. It was an autobiography called *Sailing Alone Around the World*, in which the writer did exactly what the title claimed he did. He sailed alone around the world! Not a single sailor in history was known to have done it before. And he did it in a battered old fishing sloop called the *Spray* that he took apart and rebuilt himself.

That sailor was Joshua Slocum. On 24 April 1895, Slocum cast off from Boston, in America, on his ambitious (and what many must have called hare-brained) voyage to see if he could do what he thought could be done. For three years, two months and two days, Slocum sailed 46,000 miles, stopping on different continents along the way for food and a bit of R & R—rest and repair—until he returned home famous forever.

*If Slocum could do it*, thought the young Manohar, *anyone could*. In fact, since the 1920s, others had chased after Slocum's ghost, some cutting only half an arc around the globe, some coming full circle.

When Manohar returned to India after his studies, he put Slocum out of his mind for a while as he dove into work with the Indian Navy. During the Bangladesh Liberation War of 1971, when India helped free Bangladesh from Pakistan, he captured three enemy ships and attacked a submarine. When the war ended and the dust settled, Manohar was awarded the Vir Chakra, a top award for gallantry in battle.

But in peacetime, his thoughts drifted back to Slocum . . . and to the other single-handed circumnavigators who'd followed him—Francis Chichester, Bernard Moitessier, Robin Knox-Johnston and Philippe Monnet. Manohar tracked them all, and with each journey he followed, he became more and more impatient. 'When will *we* do what the Americans, English and French have done? When will one of us sail alone around the world?'

Over the years, Manohar steadily climbed the ranks of the navy, captaining several ships, until he became the top boss of India's Western Naval Command. This is the branch of the navy that protects the waters around the western flank of the country. Now that he was in a position of power, he tried to convince the Indian government to launch the circumnavigation he had long dreamt of. He tried and he tried and he did not stop trying even after he retired from the navy in 1983.

Finally, in 2006, the blizzard of paperwork cleared, the government warmed to the idea and the mission was officially inked. It ran no longer than a complex sentence, no shorter than the circumference of the earth:

**One officer from the Indian Navy will be hand-picked and trained for a solo circumnavigation of the planet . . .**

(But there was a catch.)

**. . . on a sailing vessel made in India.**

Not only would the sailor be Indian, but the boat too!

The whole project would cost the government Rs 6.15 crore, with the boat itself running up a bill of Rs 4.5 crore. (Only a slim fraction of what it cost the government to launch India's first mission to the moon, which was over sixty times as much.)

The circumnavigation would be the ultimate test of sailor *and* boat. They'd be sailing for long, lonely months to the farthest reaches of the planet, often out of sight of land, ship or bird. Storms would snarl, seas would spit and any of many nasty things could happen: food could run out, the boat could capsize, the sailor could drown . . .

Or . . . sailor and boat *would* round the earth, and the world would clap India on the back! The country would go down in history for its heroism. It was the Indian Navy's grab at the moon. Its 'reach for the stars'. Its 'leap for land-kind'!

Of course, apart from all that glory, the mission did have another, more practical use. It would teach the navy everything they *didn't* already know about survival and navigation.

Lessons like:

 How to survive for months at sea with little food and water.

How to survive for months at sea with no one to talk to.

How to survive for months on seas that are never the same.

But most importantly: how to have a good old-fashioned, middle-of-the-ocean adventure!

A mission on the infinite waters of the rolling ocean had to have an appropriately rolling title. And so it came to be called . . .

**SAGAR PARIKRAMA . . .**

Which meant circumnavigation of the earth. On 19 August 2009, the mission weighed anchor and set off on a made-in-India sloop called the *Mhadei*, with a made-in-India skipper called Captain Dilip Donde.

Captain Donde embarked on a nine-month voyage around the world, stopping only at four far-flung ports—Fremantle, Christchurch, Falkland Islands and Cape Town—to repair the boat and replenish its stores of food, sails and spares. It turned out to be a dangerous journey, and more than once, skipper and sloop found themselves between the devil and the deep sea—which meant they were thrown into difficult situations with no easy solutions—also called fearing for your life.

But they put on their bravest faces and persevered, and on 19 May 2010, Captain Donde triumphantly steered *Mhadei* back into Mumbai Harbour to become the 190th person to sail solo around the world.

Sagar Parikrama ended up a thumping success.

The newspapers and TV channels went screaming mad with the news. The Indian Navy turned cartwheels! The Indian people jumped up in synchrony. The Indian government danced a jig. 'We've done it!' they shouted. 'We've shown the world that India too can run circles around the earth! Three cheers to us!'

All that was well and good.

But where did *I*, Lieutenant Commander Abhilash Tomy, fit in?

### Smack bang in the middle.

Now that the solo circumnavigation had gone swimmingly, the unstoppable admiral decided to raise the stakes, up the ante, double the dare. 'How about sending another Indian to circumnavigate the world alone—this time *without* stopping!' Fewer than eighty sailors in all of history had ever done it before. More people had rocketed into space (600). Many more had vaulted up Mount Everest (6000).

A non-stop sail would mean braving every peril of the sea *alone*. Without stopping at a port or flagging down a passing ship for help. It meant knowing how to set right *everything* that could go wrong, all by oneself—mending a sail, cleaning up and stitching close an open wound, sealing a crack in the hull, fixing a broken electrical device. It also meant rationing food and water to last the entire voyage. And having no other human within arm's length for days and days. In short, it was the Ultimate Survival Challenge.

*Mhadei* had already received a sound beating on her first voyage. Could she be trusted to pull off another, more punishing round? And who would be mad enough to agree to this mission, this second spin, uncomplicatedly called Sagar Parikrama II?

'Will you do it, Tomy?' the admiral's voice barrelled down the phone in December 2009. He had barely finished curving the question when the words tripped out of my mouth in their hurry to be heard: 'Yessir!'

I wasn't barking mad to agree. After all, I did have a hand in the first circumnavigation. It was I who was Captain Donde's only shore support during Sagar Parikrama, tracking his passage around the world from the naval offices in Mumbai. And didn't I, along with Ratnakar Dandekar the boatbuilder, fly to the ports where the captain had halted to help him prepare *Mhadei* for the next leg of the journey? I knew the boat like the back of my hand! In fact, I was at Lyttelton in New Zealand, attending to *Mhadei* during one of Captain Donde's halts when the admiral's call came through.

Admiral Awati knew about my lifelong hunt for adventure. He also knew how much I loved my own company. Moreover, he had watched me closely, working on *Mhadei* and other sailboats in the navy. If anyone could handle this hairy mission, he knew it was me.

*He also knew I was probably the only one mad enough to agree to it.*

And that is how I found myself at the penultimate hour of Sagar Parikrama II, preparing to do what no other Indian on a sailboat had ever done before.

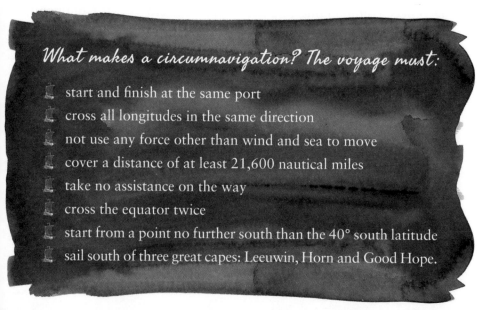

What makes a circumnavigation? The voyage must:

- start and finish at the same port
- cross all longitudes in the same direction
- not use any force other than wind and sea to move
- cover a distance of at least 21,600 nautical miles
- take no assistance on the way
- cross the equator twice
- start from a point no further south than the 40° south latitude
- sail south of three great capes: Leeuwin, Horn and Good Hope.

Out of the blue, a conch bleated like a foghorn. With a jolt, I flew back from my thoughts and landed once again at the heart of the throng at the Gateway of India. I was being summoned, by none other than the god of the sea himself. Lord Varuna. He strode barefoot on the baking squares of the Gateway jetty, his flaming orange robes and false beard flapping gaily in the breeze. Then, seating himself grandly on a blue and silver couch, he beckoned me over.

Bowing before the actor, I folded my hands and meekly asked for his blessings. 'Fair winds and following seas, my son,' he said solemnly. The crowd chuckled, tickled by the slapstick.

By now the excitement, like the heat, had thickened. The time to put out had finally arrived. I glanced at my watch. Almost noon. I walked down the jetty towards the *Mhadei*. She had started to tug at her thick mooring lines impatiently, as if to say, 'Come on, man, we haven't got all day.'

A small group of people broke away from the crowd and accompanied me to the waiting boat. In the lead was Vice Admiral Shekhar Sinha, flag officer commanding-in-chief of the Western Naval Command, the highest-ranking officer on the west coast of India. He shook me by the hand and handed me a pair of beautiful black, leather-bound binoculars and a white sea cap.

'Lieutenant Commander Tomy, you have my permission to circumnavigate the globe,' he declared ceremoniously.

I responded with a sharp salute, the military's wordless 'Yes, sir!'

After the round of hugs and handshakes with Admiral Awati, Captain Donde, Ratnakar and a few others, I turned at last to my father. He had come all the way from Kochi to see me off. I had a flashback of our goodbye in Goa all those years ago.

'Dad, it's time,' I said, trying to sound more cheerful than I felt.

'Fair winds, son,' my father replied, folding me into a tight embrace. I did not want to set off on a bleak note, but I could not close my heart to the dark possibility that this might be a journey from which I might never return. Which could make this the last time I saw my father.

Shoving the thought aside, I put on a limp smile, turned and walked briskly to the boat. Climbing over the rail, I slipped off my blue rubber slippers. From now on, I would only wear rubber-soled boat shoes or no shoes. One has to be particular about the footwear one wears on a boat to avoid slipping on water-slick decks.

Switching on the engine, I slowly motored *Mhadei* out of the marina. Once we reached the fairway buoy in the harbour—the bobbing red and white marker that told us we were in open waters—I would turn off the engine for the remainder of the journey and unfurl the sails, leaving it to the wind and current to drive me the rest of the way.

Applause erupted on land, for the mission had now well and truly begun. Applause broke out on the water too, as a flotilla of sailing boats, motorboats, a barge and even a couple of warships surfaced on the sunlit sea to see me off. Every vessel spilled over with officers, reporters, photographers and friends. Uniformed sailors stood in single file from bow to stern on the warships, doffing their caps and chanting as I passed: 'Victory to the navy! Victory to *Mhadei*.' It was a babble of muddled 'goodbyes', 'good lucks' and 'Godspeeds' that followed me, blowing tiny gusts of hope that would fill my sails for days.

Behind me, the Gateway of India started to shrink into the picture postcard the rest of the world knew it to be. I had almost reached the buoy and was about to step into open water, when suddenly I heard a motorboat puttering up, its two occupants hollering over the engine. 'Your order, Tomy,' one of the men grinned as he drew up abaft of me, holding out a square flat box.

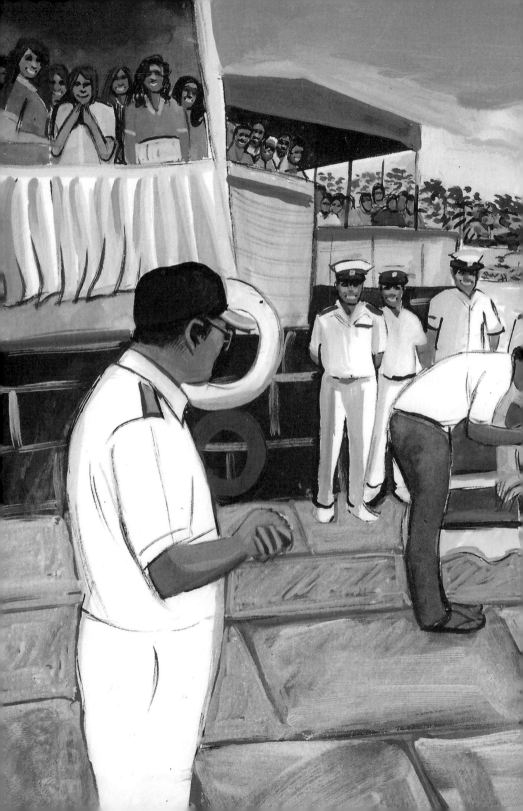

Puzzled, I reached over and grabbed it. As I threw back the lid, a cloud of steam wafted out and the herby aroma of a freshly baked pepperoni pizza filled the air, driving the fishy odour of Apollo Bunder over the boat's edge!

'Thanks, guys,' I said, chuckling.

'And thank you, old chap,' I said to the faraway friend at the Gateway, lifting a steaming slice in the general direction of the great arch, where I knew Captain Dalip K. Sharma stood watching me sail out. In the minutes before I was to leave the shore, he had pulled me aside. 'Any last requests?' he'd asked.

'I'd give my left arm for a pizza right now,' I had said distractedly. No sooner had I turned and been sucked back into the swarm, Dalip dashed across to the hotel Taj Mahal Palace behind the Gateway, stormed its Italian *ristorante* and yelled urgently for a pepperoni pizza.

'Hurry up, it's for our circumnavigating sailor. He's about to leave, come on, come on,' Dalip had shouted at the restaurant manager.

When he realized the pizza was for the man about to sail the world, the manager had it rustled up in minutes and Dalip had galloped with the hot box to a naval speedboat docked at the pier across the road! 'Compliments of the Taj', the note read.

It was my last pizza of 2012.

I wolfed it down and fished out my phone. Before I could slip out of the grasp of cell phone networks, I had one last call to make.

My mother answered on the very first ring.

'Hi, Mom,' I said. Far from the staring eyes of spectators, my voice collapsed in a heap. 'I'm off . . . It's a beautiful day . . . and I'm happy,' I said haltingly.

As far back as I can remember, my mother had always walked me to the front gate of our house in Kochi whenever I was off to school, or on picnics or to play. But this time, she refused to see me off. 'This time, I can't watch you go,' she said.

She cried for a bit. 'You know, I was listening to some prayers on the radio this morning and I heard a hymn: "Fear not the storm; God will protect you", it went. It was a sign, Abhilash. You *will* return safely. Don't ever be afraid!' she said, comforting me.

Mothers!

I spoke to her a while longer and then stowed the cell phone away. It wasn't going to ring for a very long time.

Now—I was well and truly off around the world.

## The Trishna

On 28 September 1985, a 36.6-foot yacht called the Trishna sailed out of Mumbai on India's very first circumnavigation. Its crew of ten men were not seasoned sailors, but sappers, engineers of the Indian Army. Six sailed at any given time on the west-to-east voyage, halting at over a dozen ports en route.

One of them was Major A.K. Singh.

He had lost a leg to a hang-gliding accident two years before the expedition, but, strapped with an artificial leg, went on to sail with the rest. On 10 January 1987, after 470 days at sea, the Trishna, a second-hand boat bought in the UK, returned triumphantly to the Gateway of India. The boat was later made part of the Republic Day parade in Delhi. It was also honoured with the Award of Merit by the Ocean Cruising Club, an international sailing club.

# Pulling Up a Panda

## First Leg: Mumbai to Cape Leeuwin
## 1 November 2012 to 11 December 2012

Winds blew steadily from the port quarter—the rear left side of the boat—filling up the sails and hustling the boat along. My own sails, on the other hand, had started to flag from the exertions of the day. I had much to do in the cabin below, and by the time I stepped back on deck later that evening, the last drop of blue had drained from the sky. Stretching out on the boards below the mast, I gazed up. The sky and sea were both the colour of coal, and I couldn't tell if I was up in the sky or down in the sea. Far from land's electric glare, a trillion stars shimmered like silver dust.

My eyes drifted towards a brood of bright stars called the Seven Sisters in their dome of a home. I pictured the Arabs in the East, gazing at the sisters from their desert doorways and deciding to name them *ath-Thuraya* or 'the Little Abundant One'. On the other side of the sky, the Greeks stared at the same cluster and called them the Pleiades, after the seven daughters of Atlas and Pleione, whom Zeus transformed into stars! As it happens, the first sighting of the sisters in spring marked the start of the sailing season in the Mediterranean Sea, and some say the sisters get their name from the Greek *plein*, which means 'to sail'! *Funny how words work*, I thought.

I headed down and had a light dinner of an apple because the pizza still lay heavy in my stomach. My wristwatch said 9 p.m. The electronic autopilot was working silently, keeping *Mhadei* on course. On a modern vessel like this, I could leave the tiring job of steering the boat

to the autopilot. All I had to do was set the device to a particular wind angle, and when the wind changed direction, readjust the autopilot and trim (adjust) the sails. *Mhadei* had three autopilots, two electronic and one mechanical, each a standby for the other.

Just like with an aircraft, *Mhadei* could be trusted to the autopilot, dutifully following the compass course she was set on. I would take the steering wheel to guide the boat only when we encountered a storm, or crossed crowded seas when flotsam, or other boats, or growlers— broken bits of iceberg (which were to come later)—swarmed the waters. For now, though, the waters seemed clear.

I slipped into my bunk and, within seconds, sank like a stone into a deep sleep. I couldn't have sunk very far when urgent shouts woke me up. Half-rising with a jolt, I glanced at my watch. Midnight. Hurrying up to the deck, I looked around. To the right of the boat, or the starboard side, a fishing vessel loomed out of the darkness, a fisherman standing at the bow waving frantically to me. 'Watch out for our nets!'

It turned out the waters were not as clear as I thought!

Floating on the sea like lamps were lighted buoys, each holding up the corner of a wide fishing net that hung invisibly below the water's black surface. The buoys were beacons, warning passing vessels that men and nets were silently at work there.

I shouted out an apology and, taking the wheel, steered *Mhadei* by hand out of the nets' way. Now that I was up, I decided to give the boat a quick inspection to make sure the sheets (the sail ropes) hadn't slackened. They hadn't. That done, I headed back to my bunk and slept the rest of the night in short half-hour snatches. Sleep at sea is never hours long, like it is on land.

At 7 the following morning, I checked the weather forecast on my laptop. It predicted winds blowing at 25 knots (1 knot is equal to 1 nautical mile per hour)—another day of good weather and brisk sailing. The sun had sucked the ink out of the night's water, and the sea shone a brilliant blue, its surface a mass of lively waves glinting silver where the light struck.

I made my round of the boat, checking if the rigging—the lines and cables connected to the sails and mast—were secure. If a line came undone and trailed in the water, it could get entangled in the rudder, the underwater blade that helps a vessel change direction. And should *that* happen, the rudder could get jammed and the boat would refuse to change course.

Inspecting every inspectable inch of the sailboat was a drill I had to repeat, not just every day, but several times a day. After all, it was better to catch and solve a problem when it was small and solvable, rather than wait until it turned so large it squashed you. No one better than a sailor knows, a stitch in time saves nine. (This idiom apparently originated at sea, when a small rip in a sail could grow into a long and fatal gash if left to itself.)

By 8 a.m., I sent the first of my two daily reports to the naval offices in Mumbai and Delhi. The next would be dispatched at 8 p.m. I had to do this every day too.

Work done, it was time for breakfast. Gathering a handful of butter cookies and a mug of malt, I headed up to the deck to drink in the view. Rising from the sea here and there were a few hulking ships and a scattering of fishing vessels from the villages lining the coast. I had to tread carefully to avoid the obstacle course of boats and ships and steer clear of invisible fishing lines. My experience of the night before made me doubly wary of those in particular.

~~~

People all around the rim of the Arabian Sea, from the Horn of Africa to the tail of India, have fished in its waters since before the birth of boats. What boats did, when they arrived, was allow folks to fish beyond the shallow waters that lapped the coast. First came simple reed boats and bamboo rafts that sailed close to land. Then came the dugouts, or hollowed-out tree trunks. And later canoes, the wooden planks of which were sewn together with plant fibre, and caulked or sealed with coir, cotton and a natural glue, like tree resin.

As the boats grew bolder, folks went farther out to sea, cupped by their wooden craft, the insides of which were sequined with the fallen scales of a thousand fish. All night the fishers would wait on the waters, chatting quietly and eating the flatbread, thick-grained rice and red curries they had packed for work. The following morning—or several mornings later—they'd return to shore to tip out their haul of pink shrimp, silver pomfret and purple squid, making the most delicious dunes on the beach.

When I was as high as my mother's elbow, I too fished in the streams around my father's father's house in Kuttanad, Kerala. The water rippled with the traffic of tiny anchovies. Afternoons when the whole village was asleep, I'd head down to these streams with my fishing net—a thin white cotton towel. This I'd lower into the shallow water, and patiently wait for the fish to swim into my trap. The minute they did, I'd haul up my catch and tip the towel into a glass jar, watching the silver specimens fall headlong into their new home.

The next two days would be spent in close observation. I wanted to see the anchovies eat, grow, fight—things you don't usually see them doing unless you paid attention. Sadly, I learnt very little about the private life of fish, for they would sooner die than live under watch. When I realized my studies would never reveal to me hidden anchovy behaviour, but only deplete their local population, I gave up fishing altogether.

~~~

On the fourth day, the wind changed tune without warning, becoming lazy and listless. The sea was sluggish too and lay there like a massive wet blanket. Nothing moved. I felt like I was stuck inside a still life painting, *after* the paint had long dried. There was no question about it . . . we were becalmed.

To my utter exasperation, these conditions did not change for the next couple of days. Desperate to catch the smallest passing breeze, I raised the sails every time I saw the air stir. Not only would the mainsail and genoa go up, but also the 2000-sq.-ft A3, a balloon-like gennaker used for downwind sailing—that is, sailing in the direction the wind is blowing. I called on every available sail for help.

It should be known that though they look light as paper in a picture, sails are actually monstrously heavy. Weighing almost a hundred kilos, hoisting a mainsail is like raising and lowering a giant panda on a sling . . . up and down a seven-storey building . . . with bare hands! The unwieldy gennaker itself would have taken six hands to manage on a many-handed boat, forcing me on this solo trip to summon all the strength of three strong sailors.

No fewer than three times a day, I found myself furling and unfurling the sails, so that by evening's end the energy had evaporated from my body like seawater from a salt pan. Despite my best efforts, *Mhadei* and I managed to cover a measly 40, or at best, 50 nautical miles a day, which I could have covered had I *walked* the distance! Needless to say, I was irritable and impatient. At this rate, I wouldn't even make it to the equator by the end of the year!

~~~

Now, a naval warship had been assigned to escort me out of Indian waters all the way down to Sri Lanka. Like a hulking grey-clad nanny, she stalked silently behind us as we inched down the west coast. Seeing me straining to move ahead, she hove to within 650 ft of

*Mhadei*'s stern, and with her bow to our back made as if to shoulder us forward. But what the sailors on board proceeded to do instead came dangerously close to rocking my boat.

With a great show of concern, the men waved and shouted that they knew just how to help me. Then, with exaggerated precision, they positioned a tall *pedestal fan*—like the ones at home—right at the ship's bow.

'Do you need a breeze? We'll just switch it on.'

I laughed wryly and promptly turned my back on them. Sailors too can be stand-up comics!

~~~

Even though the air was stiff as a board, the boat continued to rock gently, moved by the mechanical motion of the waves. This could spell trouble for the sails that flapped heavily with each dive and dip of the vessel. Sailors call this 'flogging', an action that could damage the leech, the fabric's long slanting edge. Putting out to sea with a worn-out sail was like trying to fly a paper plane in the rain. Definitely doomed. So I decided to take down the sails altogether until the wind reappeared. There was little else to be done, so I did little.

The sun had turned into a new fruit: the lemon of noon ripening into the orange of evening. I scooped up a pail of water from the sea and plucked two potatoes from the sling strung across the ceiling of the cabin. These I boiled in seawater. My larder was well stocked with every provision, but one—salt! The sea, I knew, would provide it by the bucketful. What the sea wouldn't provide, however, was a chopping board! I had forgotten to pack one! It was the only forgotten implement, for in planning this navigation not a single other item had been left on shore.

To prepare for my long spell on the boat, I started living in the boat months before the voyage began. Leaving my comfortable quarters in

Goa, I made myself at home in *Mhadei*'s little cabin—which was really no wider than a king-size bed—staying there from December 2011 to November 2012 . . . almost a whole year!

An important part of my preparation was working out how much fresh food I would need to take along. My rations for the expedition were: fresh food, tinned food and freeze-dried food (food that was first frozen, then vacuumed of all moisture). Fresh food would last a month; tinned would last six; and freeze-dried, up to five years. I had a fair estimate of the quantity of the last two. It was the fresh food I had to measure because it depended on how much of it I would eat, and how long it would last without spoiling.

So, during the trial run, I only stocked the boat's pantry with the fresh food I planned to carry later on—potatoes, tomatoes, cabbages and onions. As I started to cook and eat these in the quay where the boat was docked, I came to the following conclusion:

- Four kilos of potatoes would last three weeks.

- Four kilos of cabbage would also last three weeks, provided they were not cut down the middle, but peeled leaf by leaf.

- Eggs would last longer when varnished with oil. (When I actually did set sail, I opted for powdered eggs instead, which would not only survive skittish seas but would also last several years. I only prayed I wouldn't have to test their shelf life!)

Out now at sea, the larder looked positively overfed with about a hundred kilos of provisions. We had accounted for half a kilo of food consumed every day, over a course of 200 days. Optimist that I am, I hoped to return with leftovers, for I intended to tie up the ends of this expedition well before the stopwatch . . . er . . . stopped.

I sat on the bunk and ate my salted potatoes, dressed with a dollop of spicy shark pickle, a farewell gift from one of my grandfathers. As I ate,

I glanced about my spartan quarters. My bunk was on the starboard side when viewed from the stern, that is, the back of the boat. The bow was ahead of me. Four steps across the bunk was the galley or kitchen on the port side, or left of the boat. Under the floorboards where I stood to cook, was a large stash of provisions that included rice, sugar, lentils and cans of tuna.

More provisions were stored on the galley shelves, and some in boxes astern of the galley (towards the back of the boat). Also stacked here were crates of bottled water and boxes of clothes, making it my closet-cum-pantry. The compartment towards the bow was the bosun store, crammed with ropes, spare sails and other bits and bobs, while smaller storage niches for cameras, books and suchlike were set into the cabin walls. Each niche had buckled flaps to keep its contents from tumbling out. This, in sum, was the measure of my mansion—15 ft wide and 20 ft long—a handspan of a home.

The cabin had plenty of grab bars fixed to the walls so that I could steady myself when the boat heeled or rolled. Likewise, every movable object, from burner to bunk, was held in place by screws and steel bars. With all that motion on the ocean, things on a boat could hardly be expected to keep their balance!

The stove itself was gimballed, which meant it swung on pivots that kept the pots and pans perpetually level, even when the boat itself was at a steep angle. In other words, the soup wouldn't spill even when the boat rocked. To lend an extra hand and keep the stovetop vessels in place were metal clamps called pot restraints that were attached to the galley wall.

And finally, right between the bunk and the galley stood the navigation panel—the brain of the boat. This console was a vast and complex 'wall' inset with neat rows of lights, radars, gauges, dials and switches that were all part of *Mhadei*'s communication and navigational arsenal. These could pinpoint the exact coordinates of my position anywhere on the globe, forecast weather conditions, plot my course, communicate with land and send out an SOS in case things went south . . . in other words, took a turn for the worse . . . in many other words, hit rock bottom-of-the-ocean. What sailors call Davy Jones' Locker!

## Ancient Navigation Methods

Ancient sailors found their own unique ways to determine their position on the sea and chart a course to their destination—what's called navigation. Some, like the Polynesians in the Pacific Ocean, used stick charts to navigate between islands. These charts were frames of criss-crossing sticks indicating the direction of currents and pattern of waves around different islands. The islands themselves were shells tied to the frame.

Apart from their individual methods, navigators across the world followed certain universal navigational techniques, like looking to the sea and sky. They marked the position and altitude (or height above the horizon) of the sun, moon, stars and planets. These appear to move across the sky as the earth spins. Sailors measured the angle between these moving celestial bodies and the horizon, first with their bare hands, then with the help of various devices like the kamal, the cross-staff, the back-staff, the astrolabe and the sextant. A series of calculations later, they were able to determine their position at sea.

They also studied the direction of seasonal winds and ocean currents, the changing colour of the water, the appearance of clouds on the horizon and marine animals in the sea. And closer to land, they watched for familiar landforms, like mountain peaks or cliffs to guide them to shore. What's fascinating is, these techniques were often passed from one prehistoric generation of navigators to the next through stories and songs!

# A Visitor Drops in

'What in the world is this Great Wall of Woozle?!' An ancient sailor suddenly materialized in the cabin like a stowaway at mealtime. His skin, the colour of a ripe coconut, was smooth and glistening. Two black eyes, like the seeds of a sapota, squinted at the knobs and bobs on the navigation panel. I wasn't at all surprised to see him.

He stood there naked as the day he was born, and I wondered if my clothes would fit him. They wouldn't, for he was half my height and I stand five ft eleven inches tall.

'This "wall of woozle", mister, is a highly sophisticated device. Don't touch it! It uses the Global Positioning System—you know, GPS—to track a sailing path for me,' I said, as if explaining it to a simpleton. I didn't expect the man to understand half the words in that sentence, and yet I spoke them.

The fellow doubled over laughing, showing me teeth yellow as corn. 'GPS-BPS! You modern sailors couldn't find your way out of a toilet without a map. To think we only read the stars, the waves, and followed turtles and birds to discover nearly every island from Madagascar to Rapa Nui,' he said. And still chuckling, he jogged up to the deck, and diving over, disappeared into the water.

I woke up and blinked. It was midday and the sun was a sparkler in the sky, sizzling over the sea. I'd been napping on the narrow bunk in the cockpit, the cavity in the deck that leads down to the cabin. But it wasn't the heat overhead as much as the heat bouncing off the water that brought the boat to a boil. It explained why my dreams were fevered.

And peopled with ghosts.

It didn't startle me any more to see sailors I'd read about in books stepping out of their stories and standing spectrally before me ... Austronesian islanders, Indian lascars, English pirates, Arab pilots. Some would sail with me, others would whisk me back to their coasts on their canoes and ships, travelling across time quicker than sailing across a raindrop.

Alone at sea with nothing to do but keep ship, I had plenty of time to think. And my thoughts often drifted to the early days of sailing. What did the world's first sailors make of its rivers and seas? How did they gather courage to cross them? What did they sail in? What did they sail on?

The oldest known boat in the world was the Pesse canoe, named after the village in the Netherlands where it was discovered. This 10,000-year-old dugout—9.5 ft long, 1.5 ft wide—was carved out of a single log of Scots pine. Despite its astonishing durability, the thought of crouching in a scooped-out tree log with splinters pricking my bottom and the slightest swell threatening to tip me over, made my stomach turn. I patted *Mhadei*'s fibreglass hull in appreciation.

But just who were the early sailors? Scholars say they must have been humans who went out fishing about 8,00,000 years ago on wobbly rafts. Like most first inventions, their rafts may have come apart. Then again, they may have held fast and floated resolutely on the current. Had that happened, the world's first sailors would have leapt and somersaulted on their riverbanks or shores, thrilled to have discovered a way of sitting on water!

My own dream-time visitor—the one who navigated by turtle—was an ancient sailor himself. One of those intrepid Austronesians who fanned out from Taiwan, over 5000 years ago, to find and settle new homes in the Pacific and Indian Ocean, one island at a time.

We sailed too, us folk from the Indian subcontinent. And who were our sailor-ancestors? Indus Valley seamen! They crossed the Arabian Sea in flat-bottomed boats, making it as far as Mesopotamia in western Asia with gold, copper and red carnelian beads to sell in those markets. I had seen these boats myself, frozen mid-sail on stone seals and bits of pottery at the National Museum in Delhi.

I imagined myself on the deck of such a boat.

It was a clear November morning 4000 years ago, much like the clear November morning it was the day I imagined it. The sea glinted like glass and here and there, spearing up from it were the masts of small ships. My crew and I had set sail from Lothal, a port town in India, with our prow pointed towards Oman, on the other side of the Arabian Sea. With the north-east wind at our back, we flew across the water, reading the stars by night and the sun by day to keep a steady course. After days of sailing, we knew we were approaching the coast when we noticed the swells changing shape and palm fronds floating past us.

'Abhilashu,' the skipper called out to me, 'come on, man, get to work!'

I had been leaning over a wicker cage of crows, our land-finding birds, feeding them bits of my leftover lunch. The birds, or *disha-kak*, always accompanied us on our sails, even over well-worn waters, for we never knew when a rogue wind or storm would send us off course. At times like this, we'd let loose a crow. It would hover briefly over its cage, and then, with a curt flapping of its wings arrow away. If it returned to the ship in a black mood, we knew that land was still a long way off, too far for the crow to have flown without stopping to rest. But, if it did not return, we knew land was near and we'd chase after the bird, sailing in the general direction it had flown.

This time, however, we had no need for birds, for we could tell from the outline of the hills on the horizon that Oman was only a few kilometres

away (as the crow flew!). As the ship's pilot, it was my job to lead us into port. The razor rocks and reefs skulking just beneath the surface could reduce a ship to woodchips if it wasn't careful. But because I was an old hand at this and knew every anchorage from India to Arabia, I cut a clean passage through the rocks and brought the ship to berth without so much as a scratch.

Now that he had done his job, I left my Harappan figment gloating at land's lip and flew back to the present. He had only one sea to cross and I had oceans before me.

I had now been sailing for seven straight days, and on the eighth day I sailed past home: Kerala! I was too far from land to see it, but my GPS told me it lay somewhere to my left. It was close to dawn and I was adjusting the lines port quarter when I looked up and hollered 'hello' to my parents and grandparents scattered across the state. Only the waves answered.

That's when a tiny wave of homesickness washed over me. A little over 50 nautical miles separated me from my family, and all I had to do was change course and head for Kochi to be home in time for lunch. Fried pomfret and tomato curry.

Tempting though the thought was, I drowned it. I had bigger fish to fry.

The twelfth of November dawned dull and damp, when it should have been bright and electric, for it was Diwali! The sun, regrettably, was nowhere to be seen. In its place stood a swamp of brooding rain clouds. Not the best weather for a celebration, but perfect weather for something I needed more desperately—a bath. I hadn't had one in days! So when the rain fell like a long string curtain, I grabbed a bar of soap, stood out on the deck and gave myself a thorough scrubbing. The joy! I knew what an ancient relic must feel when an archaeologist chips away at its crust of mud. As for *Mhadei*, she was

relieved too, for no sooner had I bathed than she was lighter by 500 grams of grime.

Feeling infinitely refreshed, I headed down to the cabin, towelled myself dry and put on a clean pair of shorts and a T-shirt. Time for the festivities to begin.

I pulled out a vacuum-sealed, silver-foil pouch from the food crate and emptied its orange contents on a plate. Halwa. Though it smelled nothing like the sweet should have (in fact, it smelled like nothing at all), a few minutes on the fire would coax some aroma out of it. While thousands of cooks must have sweat over stovetops that Diwali, churning out tons and tons of halwa for the country, the sticky dessert in my hand was the work of a bunch of white-coated scientists bent over a Bunsen burner in a laboratory.

Not just the halwa, half my provisions had been whipped up by the Defence Food Research Laboratory (DFRL), an arm of the Defence Research and Development Organisation (DRDO). My rations included 150 packets of pre-cooked chicken biryani, lentil gravy, dal makhani, rotis and parathas, halwa, upma and rasam. Scientifically preserved and packaged, they could last months without spoiling.

So if I tore open a packet of potato parathas after a whole year, they would still be edible! Not as delicious as something freshly tossed on a hot griddle, but good enough to keep me upright. Without DFRL's ready-to-eat meals, India's armed forces would probably starve to near-death, because fresh food is hard to come by in the remote regions they're often stationed at.

After stuffing myself, I went back out on the deck to survey the scene. The day had folded up and the rain had petered out, leaving a bracing chill in the air. I scanned the horizon for passing vessels and realized I was absolutely alone on the sea. Not a flicker of light anywhere, not even the last slivers of sunlight on the water. On Diwali, people light lamps to fill their homes with hope. I did not have a lamp on board, but I wasn't about to let the day slip by without lighting the customary flame. So I headed back down and turned on the stove, and instantly a warm ring of golden light lit up the sea. On cue, the sky clapped once in a final burst of thunder, setting off a firecracker of its very own.

## Lothal

The oldest known dock in the world is at Lothal, in Gujarat, on the west coast of India. About 4300 years old, Lothal was a port town of the Indus Valley Civilization. Its excavated dock today gives us a glimpse not just into the maritime world, but into the engineering mind of this ancient culture. Measuring 700 × 120 ft, with walls of baked brick, the dock was built away from the old course of the Sabarmati River so that silt wouldn't block its inlet. It also had an outlet fitted with a sluice gate to maintain the water level in the basin. Trading ships would sail from the Arabian Sea into the Gulf of Khambhat, up the river during high tide and into the channel that led to the dock. Their cargo of gems and metals would be unloaded; the ships would be cleaned and repaired; reloaded with ivory, cotton or beads (for which Lothal was famous); and return the way they'd come.

# Crossing the Longest Line in the World

I was in the doldrums. This meant two things.

Thing One: I had reached a part of the ocean actually called the 'doldrums'. This was a belt of no, to low, winds around the equator. And what happens here? Trade winds blowing from the north-east in the northern hemisphere and from the south-east in the southern hemisphere join ranks over this hot parallel. The two embrace warmly and rise high (as warm air does), leaving not a whiff of surface wind at sea level. What this does to poor sailors and boats, like me and mine, is leaves us completely, utterly, unquestionably, comprehensively, exasperatingly S T R A N D E D! As though the hulls of our boats were glued to the water.

This region is every sailor's nightmare, for one can be marooned here for weeks. And like countless vessels before her—or alongside, stuck beyond sight—*Mhadei* floated on glassy waters like a small balloon in a large bucket! Not a single wave puckered up.

The doldrums got their name from a rude nineteenth-century word for a slow and sluggish person: 'dullard'. Today, the doldrums or Intertropical Convergence Zone goes by other names—ITCZ, *itch*, the calms—all of which describe the same static phenomenon.

Back in the day when ships had no way of sending up SOSes on radio waves, those held hostage by the doldrums were known to run out of food and water, causing some on board to fall ill and even die!

'Becalmed' was the nautical term for it, but what sailor could *be calm* when they feared imminent death!

Now even though the *itch* is hot and windless, it can be wet, for as the warm air rises, it forms a band of clouds that lets loose thunderstorms and rain on the sitting ducks down below. And it was on 17 November that I found myself in that passive position.

Naturally, frozen with no motion on the ocean brought on Thing Two: low spirits. I was in a funk!

Yet, dull days like these were leavened by routine tasks. Apart from adjusting the sails and lines and inspecting the boat over and over again, there was enough work to eat away the hours. The day began with the 7 a.m. digital weather report. It not only forecasted the weather for the next sixteen days, but also gave me a real-time view of the weather as it was shaping up, and this I studied twice a day. There was no telling when the wind would suddenly change tack, or a cyclone stray off its path and career into me. Knowing the strength and direction of the wind at every bend would tell me just where to head to fill up my sails, and what stretches of the ocean to avoid. Even so, I always plotted three course options, to use one instead of the other in case the weather turned, flighty thing that it was!

That done, I would then send a position-course-speed (PCS) report to several places at once: the War Room at the Naval Headquarters in Delhi, the Maritime Operations Centre at the Western Naval Command in Mumbai, the Indian embassies or high commissions of countries I was passing, and various Maritime Rescue Coordination Centres along the way. I also sent them other important information like updates on the condition of the boat, the weather and sightings of other vessels in the vicinity. This would help the Indian Navy keep track of my progress.

After I'd finish with the mundane tasks, I'd check my Facebook and email accounts. (Thanks to communications satellites roving the

earth, I had uninterrupted access to the internet!) As news of the voyage spread, hundreds of people started following my journey on social media. Some sent encouraging emails wishing me luck. Others wanted to know if I was lonely. And a few wrote to say they were praying for me.

One of them was a kind lady from Detroit, America, who had recently visited the Mariners' Church of Detroit, an old and beautiful building in that city. In the nineteenth century, when the church was built, poor sailors with no place to sleep or eat were welcome to spend the night and even grab a free meal there! Attaching a couple of photographs of the church with her email, the lady wrote, 'I prayed for you at the church, Abhilash. Accept these pictures as an online blessing.' As I gazed at the image on my laptop screen, of a small single-masted boat set in the red-stained glass of the church window, I felt a swell of gratitude towards all the people I had never met—and probably never would meet—who had taken the trouble to write to me and send prayers so that I would complete the circumnavigation and return home with body and boat intact.

While I was swamped with messages from around the world, there was not a blip on the home radar . . . to my enormous relief. I was happy to see my family following orders. 'I want no news at all,' I had warned my parents before leaving, determined to focus fully on the voyage without distractions from home. The last thing I wanted was a string of emails concerning which cousin was engaged to be married, and which cow had broken a horn.

But even though I had no clue about happenings on the home front, my family had front-row seats to the goings-on on the boat because of the blog I diligently wrote. Sagar Parikrama II was not just about circumnavigating the earth, but recording every bit of the adventure as it unfolded. Not only a blog, I also had to take tons of pictures and make videos whenever I could. This is why I took along a whole battery of cameras, including a Handycam, two DSLRs (with 18–50mm and 300mm lenses) and four adventure cameras to record frenzied action.

Unfortunately, the action these past days had been the exact opposite of frenzied. I had been wallowing in the doldrums for a whole week, feeling as though I was stuck between floors in an elevator.

But just when impatience began to thicken into desperation, things started to come unstuck. On the afternoon of the eighth day, a moderate 11-knot breeze whistled in. Leaping up, I grabbed hold of the wind with all my sails and hitched a ride all the way down south, towards the equator. The passage was quickened by a southward ocean current that merged ahead with an eastward equatorial current. This combined shove helped me clock 8 knots (or around 15 km/hour) in a beam reach, which meant, with the wind at right angles to the side of the boat. Although more of a canter than a gallop, at least I was finally on the move.

~~~

On 17 February 1832, a certain naturalist—who didn't yet know that a city, a mountain and an island were to be someday named after him—reluctantly girded his loins for what would be the most humiliating day of his life. Within the span of a few wretched hours, he was shaved, blindfolded, painted and dunked in water, before being paraded before the god of the sea, Neptune. From him, the naturalist had to beg permission to 'cross the line', the line being the longest latitude of them all—the equator!

The naturalist was Charles Darwin.

When the twenty-two-year-old Darwin signed up for a five-year scientific study of the rocks, fossils, plants and animals of the world aboard the British naval brig the HMS *Beagle*, he never dreamt he'd have to endure this terrifying rite of passage. It was an ordeal all those sailing across the line for the first time had to suffer. Including me.

I was twenty years old when I crossed the equator for the first time. We were cadets sailing to Madagascar on board the training squadron ship, the INS *Krishna*, when on the day of the crossing we were summoned to the deck by Lord Varuna—the Neptune of the Indian subcontinent. Dressed in a flamboyant costume, with a plastic crown perched on his head and a mace held in his hand (but without his customary crocodile chariot), it was one of my course mates who played the part of the water lord with great flourish and greater solemnity.

A series of absurd antics followed. In a pitiable show of strength, those of us crossing the equator for the first time were instructed to lift 27-kg dud ammunition shells (filled with lead instead of gunpowder). After much heaving of chest and buckling of knees, we managed to hoist these. That was the easy part.

What followed tested our gut, for we were forced to swallow the 'nectar of the gods', soma rasa. This was no sweet syrup, but a vile-looking, vile-smelling cocktail of seawater and spices! Yet, we hardened our stomachs and swilled it, for we wanted to win the sea god's favour.

But it was our costumed comrade who rewarded us for our effort. In a booming voice becoming of a god, he called us forth and presented each of us with a congratulatory certificate. Mine read:

*'We decree that our trusty and well-beloved cadet Abhilash Tomy has on this day entered our domain and has been rightly and duly initiated with all form and ceremony as our subject on board Indian naval ship* Krishna. *We do hereby charge all sharks, whales, eels, dolphins, golliwogs, pollywogs, etc., to abstain from eating, playing with or otherwise maltreating his person.'*

(A 'pollywog' is someone who crosses the equator for the first time. Once they cross over, they're called 'shellbacks'.)

Convinced this was all the guarantee they needed to step into the unknown, sailors who were poorly prepared would plunge into the heaviest of seas with a light heart, even when the wiser way to have gone in would have been with the right mind.

Folks who live off the water keep a healthy diet of superstition—for good reason. The sea, with its shifting planes and bottomless depths, can swallow a sailor from the face of the earth before the wind can draw breath. This is why fishers, pearl divers, treasure hunters and sailors pray and plead with the sea to return them safely to the grip of land, offering it hymns of praise and gifts of food. The fishers of Mumbai offer the sea coconuts, while the people of Kerala offer it rice pudding. They even knit their nets and build their boats at special times of the year and favourable hours of the day for good luck. They turn these boats into floating altars, carving gods on their keels and painting goddess eyes on their prows for protection. It is hardly surprising then that the Indian Navy's motto is 'Sham no Varuna', a Sanskrit phrase which means 'May Lord Varuna be auspicious unto us'.

## Word Origins

The word 'ocean' comes from the Greek word 'Okeanos'. This was the name of the oldest Titan child of Uranus, Sky Father and Gaia, Earth Mother. In Greek mythology, Okeanos was the god of the great River Okeanos that swept across the earth, refilling its million waterbodies. He's the father of 3000 stream spirits and 3000 ocean nymphs.

'Sea' comes via the Old English word saē, which in turn comes from the Proto-Germanic word saiwa, which means 'a large quantity of something'. The Sanskrit word for 'sea', samudra, joins two words: sama or 'coming together', and udakam or 'water'.

On 16 November, at 5.05 a.m., thirteen whole years after I stepped over it for the first time, I crossed Lord Varuna's threshold once again. But just because one has crossed the equator several times, one must never presume familiarity. Heaven knows what could happen if the sea god wasn't offered his dues. So, although I no longer had to fund my entry into his kingdom with random acts of buffoonery, I did pass into his watery mouth a capful of drink I had on board. With this peace offering, I passed unscathed into the southern hemisphere.

And just as I did, the world turned upside down.

# The Wind When It Bellows

The southern hemisphere is the land of water. Save the Arctic, the waters of the world's remaining four ocean basins are stirred together in this colossal tureen, covering 80 per cent of its surface area with liquid, and leaving the rest to dry ground. Only one-tenth of the world's population lives in the southern hemisphere, so I knew I wasn't about to encounter a sea of people! But I was about to meet traffic of another kind—trade winds.

They arrived in a rush around noon on 22 November, about 10 degrees south of the equator. As the winds gathered steam, the waves reared up, leaping and prancing like young horses that had just bolted from their stalls. We were going upwind, *into* the direction from where the wind was blowing, which was like staggering into a storm with an open umbrella pointed at its teeth. If the sailing this far had been a breeze, what I was about to encounter was half a howler.

The deeper I went into the mouth of the trades, the more sticky the sailing became. Sailing upwind is supremely difficult, not only because the boat is shoved back and sideways by the wind but also by the waves the wind whips up, sometimes almost 13 ft high—that's halfway up the neck of a full-size giraffe! The boat, in such waters, pitches up and down heavily, often vaulting up and landing back with a loud slam. It would have been easier racing a seahorse at a derby!

Each time I stepped out on the deck—which was several times a day— foam from the waves leapt up, stung my eyes with salt and drenched

me to the bone so that I was more wet than dry all through my run-in with the trades. The 23-ton vessel bounced on the water like a ping-pong ball. A landlubber would have toppled over the rail between a single rise and fall of the boat, but after spending years on shifting seas, a sailor grows sea legs *and* a sea head. Even as *Mhadei* shook like a house at the heart of an earthquake, I knew instinctively where to place my feet and how to angle my body to keep my balance on the water-slicked deck.

Now, sailing upwind requires a special kind of manoeuvring. One doesn't head directly into it like a charging bull, but sails at a 45-degree angle to it. When the wind is to the left of the boat or port side, you call this sailing on a port tack; when it's to the right, you call it sailing on a starboard tack. To sail upwind, I had to zigzag, netting just the right amount of wind in my sails to drive the boat forward. Sailing closer than 45 degrees would cause the sails to luff, which means the forward edge would flutter and slow the boat down. There was nothing much I could do in such turbulent conditions but rein *Mhadei* in, easing her down the slopes of the waves so that she wouldn't jump clean off them.

## Trade Winds

Since ancient times, sailors have clung to swift winds blowing from east to west, between 30 degrees north and south of the equator. Traders from Europe and Africa used these winds to sail towards the Americas, and from the Americas towards Asia. That's what gave them the name 'trade winds'. They are also called the easterlies because they blow from the easterly direction. Winds are always named after the direction from which they blow.

In both the northern and southern hemispheres, the easterlies don't blow in a straight line but slant a bit towards the equator. They do this because of the rotation of the earth, a phenomenon called the Coriolis effect named after French mathematician Gustave-Gaspard Coriolis (1792–1843).

In all-out murderous weather like this, I steered her by hand, and only when the seas settled did I leave her once more to the autopilot. On the bright side, all that wind wasn't wasted. The wind generator converted it into electrical energy, which was stored in the service battery bank. The electricity generated turned out to be enough to run all the boat's appliances for the next couple of days, from the navigation lights to the satellite communications system. The diesel generator, my other source of power, which usually ran four hours a day, had only to work half an hour every alternate day, now that we had this windfall.

As the days progressed, the trade winds picked up speed, going up to 30 knots, or over 55 km/hour. As captain, first, second, third mate, boatswain and cook all rolled into one, I hared about from port to starboard, stern to bow and below decks, doing single-handedly what several pairs of hands would have done on an ordinary sail—reefing and unreeling the mainsail, securing the lines *and* whipping up dinner.

By the time the winds finally piped down, I was knocked out as though I'd been dealt a zinger at a boxing match. I flopped on the bunk and fell into the black hole of sleep, certain I wouldn't wake up for a hundred years.

I woke up two hours later.

Out of habit. It was around 3 in the morning and the winds had momentarily died down. I went up to the cockpit and sat there for a while. The moon waxed full and bright like a spotlight, bathing the sea in a milky glow. The only sounds were the susurration of the waves and the flapping of the sails. For acres and acres around, there was nothing but water and sky.

*Alone, alone, all alone,*

*Alone on a wide, wide sea!*

I felt like I was floating inside an inkwell. But I wasn't lonely. I basked in the peace and solitude, enjoying the company of nature. It was the paradise I'd always dreamt of, and the double percussion of wind and waves was music to my ears.

I was so intent on it, I didn't hear a new note breaking in—the tiny flop of something hitting the deck. A couple of somethings. *Flop. Flop. Flop. Flop. Flop.*

Only the following morning, on my routine inspection of the boat, did I discover what it was—flying fish. Five of them lay scattered on the deck. Their narrow torpedo bodies, no longer than my hand, gleamed dully in the sun and their large silver winglike fins lay limp by their side. It was the first breakfast the sea had served up, and I should have said 'thank you'. But flying fish are so bony, I'd have been better off chewing a pincushion! I picked up each dead fish and threw it back into the sea, with a polite 'Thanks, but no thanks. Make the next lot mackerel, please.'

Some people believe the water across the five ocean basins (covering a whopping 350 million sq. km of the planet!) is all the same liquid. *Water, water everywhere, and everywhere the same.* But that's like saying all land is made up of the same soil. Depending on what parts of the planet they occupy, seas and oceans are as different as Siberia and the Sahara. Closer to the ice caps, the water is colder than water closer to the equator. The water at the ocean's surface is warmer than water at its bottom. And some parts are saltier than others. It is because of this difference that the plant and animal life in different ocean basins is like chalk and cheese . . . or like parrotfish and pricklebacks (the former found in the tropics, the latter in northern seas!).

In 1751, a British captain called Harry Ellis discovered that water in one spot of the ocean changes as you go deeper into its depths, when he lowered a bucket down the side of his ship off the coast of

West Africa. He spent quite a bit of rope on its descent, and when he drew the bucket up, he found to his surprise that the water was colder down below than it was at the surface.

This is because of the deep currents that flow in loops across ocean basins, transferring cold, dense water from the polar regions to equatorial waters, and taking their warm waters the other way around. Captain Ellis may not have known how to explain the temperature difference, but he did know what to do with the cold water—he used it to cool his wine.

I did not need to fetch far down for refrigeration because a chill was setting in the air itself. After a little over a week wrestling the trades, I was now at the threshold of the Tropic of Capricorn, about to leave the tropical Indian Ocean through its back door and approach the temperate Southern Ocean through its front.

To prepare for what was to soon turn into icy weather—with temperatures plummeting to 'deep freeze'—I dug into my stock of winter gear that included the thick fleece jacket, oilies (the waterproof oilskin jacket and trousers), heavy leather boots and sleeping bag. I needed the sleeping bag because the bare bunk would be cold comfort.

But before the chill arrived, on 1 December came another augur of new waters—a magnificent specimen of the brown Antipodean albatross.

Led by its pink pointer of a bill, the bird floated into view one afternoon, its broad white wings hooked on air currents. The wings were outstretched and unmoving, making the albatross seem more seaplane than seabird.

I was standing at the stern gazing up at the newcomer, when a grizzled old man with skin like cracked leather and a beard like a tangled fishing net took form right next to me. Around his shrivelled neck hung a limp weathered chord. He too held the albatross with a glittering eye. I knew him at once (because, of course, he had stepped out of my own brain).

It was the Ancient Mariner.

The Ancient Mariner is the ill-fated hero of Samuel Taylor Coleridge's famous poem 'The Rime of the Ancient Mariner'. He's a sailor who sets off with a full crew of men on a long voyage. All goes well until the ship is driven by a storm into the icy Southern Ocean. Out of the blue, an albatross starts to fly with the ship, like a guiding spirit. One day, without reason, the Mariner shoots the bird. At first, his companions are livid and curse him because they believe it was the bird that brought the wind that sailed the ship. But then, the fog that had enveloped the ship lifts and they now praise the mariner, convinced it was the bird that had brought the fog. (What vacillators!). And when the ship is stuck fast on a windless sea, they change their minds again and curse him once more, this time going so far as to hang the dead albatross around his neck as punishment!

I look with sympathy at the man on my boat, his back curved like a question mark. *That albatross must have weighed at least ten kilos!* I thought to myself.

'For nearly 200 years, this bird has hung about my neck!' the Ancient Mariner moaned in a reedy voice. 'You think I'm free of it at the end of the poem, but no! . . . Did you read the poem to the very end, by the way?' he suddenly asked me. 'It's rather long.'

'Yes,' I said, 'I know what happens at the end.'

'And yet, even though it has been read and recited and recited and read, no one gets it! All life on Earth, from ant to albatross, has to be preserved and protected, not destroyed like I stupidly did. Now look what's happened to me! Each time a defenceless creature is killed for

no good reason, that bird you see up there swoops down again and reattaches itself to my gullet.'

No sooner had he said it, the albatross stopped circling overhead and dove soundlessly towards us. It perched on the gunwale to catch its breath, and then before I saw how it did it, fastened itself to the Mariner's cord like a pendulous pendant. Gnashing his teeth, the Mariner let out a howl long as his poem.

What could I say to him, a figment of my imagination!

I would have stayed and commiserated with the long-suffering Mariner, but I had to turn my attention to a more urgent matter, so I headed to the cabin. Even though the trades were safely behind us by now, waiting just around the corner was a far worse fury, and we were about to pass through its teeth—the Roaring Forties!

# Laundry Day

The Roaring Forties, between the latitudes of 40 and 50 degrees, is where the winds do exactly what their nickname says: they roar! With little land mass to slow them this far down in the southern hemisphere—save a part of South America, Australia and New Zealand—the westerlies run wild across the water, churning up waves into jagged cliffs!

Gales and storms are frequent visitors here, and a sailboat unlucky to get caught in them would be wise to remember the old sailor's saying: 'No laws 40 degrees south, no rules 50 degrees south, no gods 60 degrees south!' I was still well above the sixtieth parallel but I decided, should things get ugly, I would offer every prayer I knew to any god within earshot. (They also say, 'no common sense 70 degrees south', but I had sense enough to stay way above *that* line).

A week before I met mean weather, I briefly entered a plain of quiet seas where I was becalmed once more. Located at about 30 degrees north and south of the equator, these high-pressure zones are where winds go in one of two directions, either flying towards the equator as trade winds or towards the poles as prevailing westerlies. What's left behind is no wind. The region is also called the horse latitudes.

Some of the most picturesque words and phrases I knew came from sailing and told fascinating stories about life at sea. Take 'horse latitudes', for example. They got their name from a rather gruesome old practice.

That was when trading ships heading to the Americas carried horses on board to be sold on the continents. When these ships were becalmed in this region, often for weeks on end (much like in the doldrums), food resources would dwindle and horses would starve and die. The sailors had no choice but to throw their bodies into the sea. And that's the grim story behind this name.

Knowing that the road ahead was going to be a rough one, I wanted to make the most of the brief lull before the storm. I wrote my blog and gave the boat a thorough look-over to make sure everything was working smoothly. Then I settled down to eat a warm meal.

My rations on board were meant to match weather conditions, the principle being:

- Good weather: cook and eat.
- Moderately bad weather: heat and eat.
- Weather you would only wish upon your maths teacher: unwrap a snack bar!

Knowing I would soon be lunching on nothing but snack bars, I treated myself to a plate of hot chicken biryani from the DFRL buffet. All I had to do was tip its contents into a saucepan and turn on the stove.

After my meal, I decided to do the laundry, so I ran my clothes through the washing machine. And where was this handy device? All around the boat, of course! The ocean itself!

## Ocean Laundry 101: How to Wash Your Clothes in the Big Blue

*Step 1* Soak clothes in a plastic bucket with a handful of detergent.

*Step 2* Tie bucket to a rope.

*Step 3* Fix rope to stern.

*Step 4* Lower bucket into water.

*Step 5* Let boat barrel ahead, dragging 'clothesline' behind it.

*Step 6* Wait 10 minutes. Pull up rinsed clothes.

*Step 7* Spread on deck to dry.

*Step 8* Once dry (if a bit stiff), fold clothes and stow away.

(Incidentally, sailors actually refer to rough sailing conditions as 'washing machine' conditions.)

Chores complete, boat and sailor tuned and primed, I felt we were now as ready as we could possibly be for whatever lay ahead. (Although, as far as the ocean is concerned, it's only *after* you're out of it that you know if you were prepared when you went in!)

On 6 December, the Roaring Forties came hurtling in over the horizon. The wind wheeled at 35 knots like a car in fifth gear, roiling the waves until they swelled with rage, dark as tar and tall as steeples. They rose and fell and rose and fell, some crashing directly on the boat, others pulling up the ground from under her hull, so that poor *Mhadei* pitched forward and back, and heeled dangerously to the side like a bull bitten by a bee. It was all I could do to stay on my feet

inside the cabin. Shrieking, the wind nicked off the white fringes of the waves and hurled them into the air, making it seem like we were sailing through stinging confetti.

What a warm welcome by a cold ocean!

I had prepared for the blast the previous evening by unfurling the staysail and taking three reefs on the mainsail (that is, partly closing it). I knew I'd have more than enough wind to take me a long way without the main in full flap. But such was the wind's strength that it pulled apart the pad eye of the runner block. This is the metal loop that secures the block, or pulley, through which the ropes of the sails are fastened. I quickly reattached the ropes to another block and took down the staysail.

As if one problem a day wasn't enough, a couple of hours later the wind vane autopilot gave up the ghost. Instructed by the wind, this mechanical device at the stern steered the boat. Only now it would not, because the wind, in a temper, had pulled apart the weather vane's ropes, dismantling the whole system. This meant the thing was utterly useless.

Had I been a man without a plan, I would have been forced to steer the boat by hand. Joshua Slocum did it on the *Spray*. But this was not recommended because I had a couple of months of non-stop sailing ahead of me and needed to conserve my energy for other tasks. (Slocum wasn't always at the wheel, by the way. He often lashed it with ropes to keep a steady course, while he cooked lunch or napped in his cabin.) Fortunately, I did have a plan. Not one, but two. These were the boat's two electronic autopilots which, being pressed into duty, would steer *Mhadei* the rest of the way.

Over the last stretches of the Indian Ocean, the wind chased us out with a club in hand. But even with my heart closer to my mouth than my chest, I was struck dumb by its brute beauty. The water bubbled and boiled and turned a shade of royal blue I had never seen before, even as wave upon wave piled on top of each other, one moment lifting us to show us the world, and flinging us down the next into canyons that blotted out the sun.

But *Mhadei* flew right through it, gobbling nautical miles at the rate of almost 200 a day! We had now been out at sea for thirty-seven days and had crossed 5100 miles off the chart. For three whole days, we were battered by the Roaring Forties, until finally the winds let out one final gasp and fell in a heap. It was our first gale of the voyage, and I was grateful to get out of it with my teeth still in my mouth.

But even though the wind had gone quiet, it had stirred horribly tall seas that sighed heavily with swells that rose to the height of basketball hoops. Swells are long, rounded surface waves, set off by strong winds or distant storms. They start thousands of miles away and lumber across whole oceans! Now, while swells are not hysterical like waves in a storm, they are no less infernal. *Mhadei* rolled drunkenly from side to side on the swell that came in from the south-west and turned her cabin inside out. Onions spun like marbles in every corner; malt from an upturned mug made a moving map across the floor; and under the bunk lay one of my cameras, with internal injuries it wouldn't even speak of.

Afraid of what the combined effect of swell and light wind would do to the rigging, I took down all the sails (they were up again by now) except for the A3, the gennaker that controlled the wind in unstable conditions like these. From then on, it was (relatively) smooth sailing till 115.14° east, the longitude of our first Great Cape—Leeuwin. On 12 December 2012, I flew across that line, breaking past the first ribbon of our 23,000-nautical-mile marathon.

The first leg of the expedition had been successfully completed!

## Food

Today, you can dig into all kinds of delicious food on a boat, from tandoori chicken to chocolate millefeuille, thanks to refrigeration and modern kitchens on board. But there was a time when sailors were lucky to be served anything other than hard tack.

Hard tack was a rock-hard biscuit made of wheat flour. So tough, they were also called molar breakers and could only be bitten after dunking them into hot coffee or water. But because they were reasonably nutritious and had a long shelf life, they became a sailing staple.

Fresh food and water wouldn't last long if the journey took months, so only rations unlikely to spoil quickly in sea air (and water) made it into the hold. Indian sailors carried rice, wheat, pulses, ghee and butter, sugar, honey, pickles and dried fruit. Some ate salted fish; others, salted meat. Salt helped preserve food.

Yet, whenever they craved fresh fare, sailors dropped a fishing line over the gunwale or dropped anchor along the way to hunt game on land. Chinese fleets of the Ming dynasty actually grew food on board! By sprouting soya bean and planting ginger in pots, they made sure they not only had fresh food but also a steady supply of Vitamin C, of which ginger root is a rich source. The deficiency of this vital vitamin is what caused countless sailors to die of scurvy at sea.

Mariners in the Pacific would make pitstops at the Galapagos Islands for turtles. Because turtles can survive up to a year without water, these animals would be stowed in the ship's hold and served up as steak later in the journey. Other provisions included cheese, onions, beans and peas.

As for drinking water (for this also went bad), various containers were used in different parts of the world. Arabian sailors carried freshwater in tall ceramic jars or amphorae. Indians stored their water in deep wooden troughs. In many parts of the world, beer was also a staple. All food and water were carefully rationed to make supplies last and keep every sailor fed (even if not always well fed).

# A River for a Boat

There was once a Great White Whale called Jeedara, created to protect Earth's ocean. He swam in from the Milky Way in the sky. As he swam, the Pleiades, the Seven Sisters, sang out to him, calling Jeedara over to them. But the Great White Whale wouldn't go. Stung, the sisters threw a rock at him. Seething, Jeedara gave chase, slicing through the water like a lightning bolt. Such was his strength that the waters split up and the ocean floor trembled and cracked. Part of it started to bank up, higher and higher still, until it pushed clean past the surface and only stopped halfway to heaven.

There it still stands, a colossal wall of rock, sheer and unbroken, the longest cliff line of its kind in the world. The Bunda Cliffs.

Rising as high as 330 ft, the cliffs snake across the southernmost part of Australia for about 100 km. And at their feet, they cup a rolling C-shaped bay called the Great Australian Bight. Into this bay, every Australian winter, swim the southern right whales, an endangered species that come here to nurse their newborn calves until they're strong enough to swim back into the colder seas of Antarctica. It's why the Great Australian Bight is one of the greatest whale nurseries in the world!

To the Mirning people, the indigenous tribe that lives in this region, the southern right whales are the descendants of the Great White Whale, Jeedara. They worship and sing sacred songs to them, and work very

hard to keep the Great Australian Bight clean and sheltered so that the whales have a safe place to raise their young.

On the twelfth day of the twelfth month of the twelfth year of the twenty-first century (that's '12' reversed!), I sailed into the Great Australian Bight.

December is summertime in Australia. Had I been sailing in the winter of June, I would have spotted the great-great-to-the-power-of-∞ grandchildren of the Great White Whale, trumpeting their arrival with sprays of silver mist. I pitched my mind several months ahead. There I'd be, bobbing blissfully in my little boat on the smooth blue waters . . . when a leviathan would glide darkly in my direction, inches below the surface. Then, without so much as a 'Do you mind?' or 'Have you room?' the whale would leap clean out of the water and land squarely in my lap, taking boat and me to the bottom of the sea.

The thought thrilled me.

As it happened, it wasn't a shape in the water, but something out of thin air that livened things up that December day—emails. They arrived in quick succession in my mailbox, each from a member of the Sagar Parikrama core team: Admiral Awati, Captain Dilip Donde and Ratnakar Dandekar, the boatbuilder. All congratulations and warm wishes . . . not for me, but for the boat! For it was on 12 December 2008, exactly four years ago, that *Mhadei* had had her first taste of water. Which is something of a big deal.

It was her launching day when her hull was lowered with many prayers and much fanfare into the Mandovi River. A boat's launching day is like a person's birthday, but instead of cake smeared on the face, a bottle of wine or champagne is cracked against its hull. If the bottle does not break on the first try, the boat is believed to be doomed! In India, a new boat receives a knock from something far tougher than a wine bottle—a ripe coconut!

The calendar read 12/12/12. *Mhadei*'s anniversary would never see such immaculate sequencing again.

I was introduced to *Mhadei* in April 2009, when I was appointed Commander Donde's shore support in the first round of the circumnavigation. Now while it was he who completed that mission, it was the boat that kept him afloat. Several Indian boat-builders had hoped to snag the prestigious (if risky) project, but it was eventually Ratnakar who won the bid to build the boat in December 2007.

Ratnakar ran his boatbuilding business, Aquarius Fibreglas, from a remote corner of an island in Goa called Divar, on the Mandovi River. Incredibly, the island itself is shaped like a sailboat, with its prow nosing the Arabian Sea, and its stern backing into the mainland! One of the last few redoubts in Goa, you can visit it only by ferry. It was at this little boatyard that Ratnakar started to construct the most important boat he had ever built in his life.

It took fourteen months to piece her together with state-of-the-art parts sourced from all around the world: sails from Sri Lanka, mast and rigging from South Africa, engine from Sweden, generator from the Netherlands, water maker from Italy, galley from the United States and red cedar wood for the hull from Kerala. After the last screw had been turned and the final lick of paint dried, all that was left was to give her a name.

~~~

If the boat's birthplace, the river Mandovi, were to be traced all the way back to its starting point, that point would be in Karnataka. There, the river is known by another name: *Mahadayi*. But as she winds her way from Karnataka into Goa through the wooded Sattari Valley between the two states, she acquires yet another name.

It was this name that Admiral Awati discovered one afternoon when he entered the Sattari forest. Deep in the woods, he was led to a couple of black basalt slabs from another time, propped up on the forest floor. Carved into the slabs was the figure of a lady on the deck of a boat, flanked by oarsmen. Above her, in the crow's nest—the lookout high up on the mast—were caged *disha-kak*, land-finding birds. The lady was none other than the river goddess Mhadei, the patron deity of the local people. *Mahadayi, Mhadei, Mandovi.*

'My search for a name for our circumnavigating boat has come to an end,' the vice admiral had declared. 'She will be called *Mhadei*!'

All great rivers meet the sea, but *Mhadei* was destined to go farther. She would meet and circle the great global ocean.

~~~

'Shore support, we've got a problem! The diesel generator broke down.'

We were still sailing along the 40th parallel south, heading for light winds further up the path when the generator started to throw a fit, jumping to life, then playing dead every ten seconds. The generator was *Mhadei*'s main source of electricity, not to mention a reliable one. The other two sources, the solar panels and wind generator worked only if there was sufficient sun or wind. I fed the machine a quantity of engine oil and even attempted some rudimentary servicing, but nothing worked.

Exasperated, I finally emailed the manufacturing company for help. 'It's probably a sensor issue. Replace the sensor,' they prescribed. But I had no spares. So I cleaned the old sensor well and fitted it back into place. What do you know! It worked! The generator rumbled to life and rumbled well beyond ten seconds.

Life at sea was never dull. There was always something to do . . . or puzzle over. One morning, for example, I noticed feathers scattered like snow inside the cabin. Could a bird have accidentally flown in? I started to search the boat for the stowaway, when my eyes finally found the fiend. It was my sleeping bag! There was a large tear in its lining and it was from this that the feathery stuffing had spilled out and scattered around the boat.

After cleaning up the mess, straightening up the cabin and sewing up the lining, I threw myself a feast for my hard work—fried sardines. Now, per my provisioning, canned food was reserved for weather worse than the minor buffeting I had been experiencing. But sometimes you just have to throw caution—and your meal plan—to the wind. I peeled open the can and threw the fish on the skillet, watching it sizzle in hot oil until it was crisp and brown. This I took up to my favourite perch, the cockpit, and made a slow and mincing meal of it.

The early evening sky was now a quilt of heavy greys. Clouds hung low and the daytime temperature was a cool 20°C. Despite this, my forehead and back were sequined with sweat. Perhaps the thick layer of grime I wore like a boiler suit was insulating me against the chill, I reasoned. After all, my last bath was two weeks ago! It was a good thing my mother wasn't my officer of the watch.

But the grime was too much, even for me, so after my meal, I headed for a shower. Being a compact vessel, everything on the boat was a compressed version of itself, including the shower cubicle, which was about as spacious as a drainpipe. In addition to the health faucet that doubled as a showerhead, it had just enough room for a tiny washbasin and a toilet. Naturally, bathing or . . . er . . . relieving bodily burden, demanded dexterous yogic ability. But if I could shimmy barefoot up the mast on rocky waters, what were a couple of simple bathroom contortions!

Now, all organic waste generated on a boat—whether of the belly or the galley—can be emptied into the sea. Fruit, vegetable peels and food leftovers I simply tipped over the gunwale, while the toilet too purged its waste, called black water, directly but more discreetly, into the blue. All of this would biodegrade naturally. But trash like used foil packets, tins or anything else that would pollute the ocean had to be stored in bin liners on the boat, to be disposed of responsibly when I reached the shore.

## Ocean Currents and the Great Ocean Conveyor Belt

Water in the global ocean never stays put like water in a pail. It constantly circulates—not just across the length and breadth of ocean basins, but also from their surface to their depth. Different parts of the global ocean flow in fixed directions, forming currents. The largest of these is the Antarctic Circumpolar Current.

Now, there's a method in the way currents move, and it depends on wind and water density. Prevailing winds that blow in fixed directions in different regions of the earth—like the westerlies and easterlies (trade winds)—move water across the ocean's surface. These form surface currents. Try blowing a drop of water across a table to get an idea.

On the other hand, there are also deep ocean currents at play. Here's how they work: When water is cold or salty (like around the poles), it becomes heavy or dense. Dense water sinks to the bottom of the ocean, making room for warmer, less dense water that travels in from another part of the ocean (like say, the equator). When this water cools in turn (for it has entered a colder region), it too becomes dense and sinks. This constant rising and sinking forms cycles of currents across different ocean basins.

Both surface and deep currents work like a global delivery system, transferring heat and nutrients across the global ocean. It's why it's called the global conveyor belt. (By the way, the global conveyor belt is not as quick as you think. It would take a drop of water 2000 years to travel the global ocean.) It may be slow but it is life-saving, for this nifty system not only controls the temperature of the ocean but also the climate on Earth, and by doing so, it supports all life on the planet.

# Deep Freeze

It was early evening when I set about doing what I usually did at that time in those days—grazing cows. I was ten years old. My grandfather, Philip, with whom I spent my summer holidays in Nedumkunnam, Kerala, was a man of few but fixed beliefs. One of these was that no child must ever be heard to say 'I'm bored'. Especially during their summer vacation. That, according to him, meant the child was plain lazy. For there was always something to think about. And if there was absolutely nothing to think about (impossible!), there was always something to do. To make sure those words never left my mouth, let alone enter my head, he set me a daily list of chores.

These included, but were not limited to:

- delivering the morning's newspaper to the neighbours
- gathering twigs for the kitchen fire
- slicing jackfruit for breakfast
- helping my grandmother, Anne, carry the dirty laundry to the stream
- accompanying my grandfather to his rubber grove, where he drained the trees of their sticky white latex, to be sold later to rubber manufacturers
- driving the cows out to graze
- drawing water from the well several times a day
- shooing hens from the front yard several times an hour.

The particular evening I took the cows to lunch was a blisteringly hot day. I rested against a warm rock under the rooted shade of a banyan tree, with one eye on the cows and the other on a crow's nest overhead. I would have nodded off to sleep were it not for what happened next.

The weather began to turn before my very eyes. A small wind crept in at first, gently cuffing the cows' ears. Within minutes, on the back of this breeze strode a larger wind that swept up their tails. Before the hour was out, the yellow day turned to steely twilight and a chill crept in, frosting my open toes.

The wind had now started to howl. It bent the spines of the coconut trees, and swirled up the dust so that there was little of it left on the ground. The long grass of the paddy nearly flew off their fields, and overhead electricity cables swung like skipping ropes. Leaving the cows to their fate, I scampered home, terrified. By the time I reached my grandparents' front gate, my lungs were on fire. Then, just as I was about to run up the path that led to the house . . . down with a sickening thud fell the largest, ripest, prickliest jackfruit that had ever sprung from a tree. The wind had violently knocked it down. Any closer and the blow would have landed squarely, and perhaps fatally, on my skull.

That day, as I gaped with horror at the yellow flesh of the fractured fruit, I read the writing plain on the wind: *Don't take me for a breeze, boy. I can ruffle your hair, but just as soon split your head wide open.*

It was a warning I would never forget.

~~~

It was four days to Christmas. But instead of angels singing, I could only hear the caterwauling of cats. They came racing across a crumpled sea as westerly tailwinds at 45 knots, or 83 km/hour. Alongside came our old friend, the swell from the south-west. Cold seawater swept over the deck and spilled back out as the vessel rolled from side to side. Definitely not the weather for still-life painting.

I hadn't planned to sail south this early in the game, but I had to change plans at the last minute to escape the headwinds brought about by an occlusion (when two masses of cold air collide, one colder than the other). This clash of two air masses of different temperatures and humidity is also called a front. Tagging behind it are rain and storms. As I dove down the parallels in worsening weather, I drew closer and closer to that band of hair-raising winds between latitudes 50° and 60° south, fondly called the Furious Fifties.

If the Roaring Forties had a temper, the Furious Fifties were howling mad. The wind scorched about the Southern Ocean like a cat at a mouse convention. The Australians make no joke when they say these winds can blow the roof right off a house and a dog straight off its chain! It has been known to happen.

At 50° south, I was closer to the South Pole than I was to the equator, and the weather made sure I knew it. I was cold and wet, and the boat was wet and cold, both inside and out. My bunk was hardly ever dry, so I was forced to sleep on what couldn't have been all that different from the top rack of a refrigerator. Things were either damp or soaking wet, and I had no choice but to bear it grimly. Despite the oilies and the visor to protect my face from the spitting sea, ice-cold water trickled between the layers, leaving me uncomfortable and frozen throughout.

Contributing magnanimously to this vacation weather were the waves that made the boat jounce about like a dice on a board game. They crashed over the deck and each time they struck me, my fingers and brain recoiled like a wound from salt.

In the middle of this siege came a timely message from Admiral Awati: 'Bash on regardless.' *Was he talking to the waves or to me?* I wondered. Regardless, I did bash on—for two whole days—and managed to stay afloat with both, the hull and my head unbroken.

By now, I was padded in full winter gear, what with daytime temperatures hovering between 7°C and 10°C, and falling to 'I-can't-feel-my-face' degrees at nightfall. I wore thick gloves and sailing boots at all times and a diver's face mask to keep my jaws from unhinging. But despite the heavy gear, I did catch the sniffles. Interestingly, a story goes that midshipmen—young sailors training to be officers—missed their homes so much, they moped and snivelled out at sea, wiping their runny noses on their cuffs. To discourage this snotty practice, the navy insisted that buttons be sewn on cuffs. (This story sounds decidedly dodgy, for couldn't the men wipe their noses elsewhere on their sleeves?)

New Zealand was now 30 nautical miles to my north. I thought of my brother Aneesh who lived there, as I stood soaking wet at the stern, clammy hands on the steering wheel, chattering teeth in my head. Surely he was warmer than I, wherever he was.

Most people warm themselves indoors in such weather. But a cabin hatch and fibreglass are poor defence against the spearing chill at sea. Touching any metal with bare hands, be it the winches or its handles, the mast, the handholds, the guard rails—even a spoon—resulted in a sharp sting, like touching a live wire. Even my thoughts turned cold! They drifted up and out of my mind in white condensed clouds. Should another boat have come by, I was sure I could signal them with vapour words like Native American smoke rings!

Unfortunately, I couldn't test this new ability. I was near the Southern Ocean after all, and the odds of spotting another human in this wet desert were far lower than spotting one in outer space. The only people to cross these latitudes were the daredevil single-handed sailors of races like the Vendée Globe and the Velux 5 Oceans Race, competitions so exhausting and dangerous, they take place only once every couple of years.

The other vessels to brave these waters were megaton tankers and cargo carriers, but these too were rare sightings. The near-constant stormy conditions of the Southern Ocean cost many sailors their lives here, so it wasn't an overripe imagination that gave this stretch the eerie name 'Dead Men's Road'.

## Big Chill

Did you know that 10 per cent of Earth's land area is covered in glacial ice? And 90 per cent of that ice is in Antarctica? The rest covers the Greenland ice cap. (Glacial ice is ice that sits on land, not the kind floating in water—that's sea ice.) But these numbers are rapidly changing, for the ice itself is melting rapidly, because the earth is warming so fast. This is catastrophic! For one, it causes sea levels to rise and coasts to be eaten away, endangering all life on coastlines: human, plant and animal. Its effects will gradually be felt inland as well.

Melting ice also disrupts the flow of ocean currents, which can disrupt the distribution of food in the ocean and affect the temperature and salinity of the water. This threatens life within the ocean as well. And because ocean currents help control temperatures above water too, any change in the currents could also spell change in climate patterns, with more heatwaves, storms and cyclones headed our way. So, although glaciers seem very far off, they are more closely connected to us than we think.

# Christmas at Sea

For many centuries, people living north of the equator had a fairly good idea about what lay to the south of it—even though they had never stepped foot there themselves. They speculated that a large continent must lie in the southern hemisphere to counterbalance all that land on the other side . . . like two pans on a weighing scale. Without this 'Great South Land' for balance, Earth would topple over like a top-heavy ball and roll right into the cosmic abyss.

Little did they realize that the great mass of land they imagined was, in fact, a great mass of water, forming the southern Atlantic, the southern Pacific, the southern Indian, and the Southern (or Antarctic) Ocean itself—the southernmost of them all. And at the heart of this hemisphere lay Antarctica, the world's largest desert, a white cloud of a continent 14.2 million sq. km in area, or about four times the size of India.

As I sailed past the fifty-third parallel of the southern hemisphere, I felt like I was slipping all the way down to the bottom of the earth. This was the farthest south I had travelled so far, and I had half a mind to go on sailing right to the Antarctic Circle, which was only 13 latitudes away.

Despite the acres and acres of leaden sky and sea that surrounded me, I was in high spirits, because we had just skirted a storm brewing to the north of us! The weather forecast had warned of its coming, so we prudently slowed down and allowed the low-pressure system to rattle by without getting in its way. A low-pressure system is a spinning mass of moist, warm air that causes strong winds and storms. Now that it had passed, it was going to be slow and easy sailing for the next couple of days.

There was another reason I was buoyant as a booby. Christmas was around the bend.

On Christmas Eve, the sun surfaced just before noon. It broke warm and yellow like an egg yolk in what had until now been a charred skillet of a sky. After Diwali, Christmas was to be my second celebration at sea and it was time again to lay out the smorgasbord. So I rummaged through the rations and drew up a wholesome packet of freeze-dried vegetables! Somehow, frozen vegetables didn't quite spell 'holiday spread', so I threw in a can of cola and half a bar of dark chocolate, and then it was a feast!

It was a good thing I had had my Christmas banquet the day before, because 25 December turned out to be a damp squib! The clouds went into a huddle overhead, not a single ray of sunshine made it through and the seas grew more violent as I rode the waves up north.

Winds topping 30 knots chased the boat and raised the seas so that I found myself tied to the steering wheel all day. And as I stood at the helm, chilled to the marrow, in what was an utterly cheerless spot to be on Christmas, a Christmas story came to mind.

On 22 November 1912, a floating forest of Christmas trees sailed across Lake Michigan in the United States. There they were, a couple of thousands of them plucked clean off the ground and squeezed tight into the hold and deck of a three-masted schooner. The name of this ship was the *Rouse Simmons* and its captain was Herman E. Schuenemann.

Every winter, Schuenemann would sail up the Chicago River selling Christmas trees. His ship would barely fasten its moorings on the bollards lining the quay when impatient crowds waiting on the docks would course up the gangplank, eager to find the best evergreen on board. The ship itself looked like a bristling Christmas store. Electric lights decked it from end to end, and alongside the trees sat sailors and their families selling wreaths, bunting and other decorations they'd hand-crafted themselves.

Now, Captain Schuenemann was a kind man who often gifted trees to poor folk who couldn't afford them. And for his generosity, they nicknamed him 'Captain Santa'.

That November, the crowds waited as always for the Christmas Tree Ship and Captain Santa to turn up. But one day passed, and then another, and then several, but neither arrived.

Only later did people learn what had happened. A terrible gale had broken out on Lake Michigan on the afternoon of 23 November; a storm so terrible it blanketed the air with snow and mist and angrily stirred up the waters. The floating forest did its best to stay afloat. But after a long and wrenching battle with the sea, it capitulated and sank without a trace . . . taking Captain Santa with it.

Christmas everywhere else came and went, but on the dark waters of Lake Michigan, it stayed for weeks and months. For every once in a while, a tree would break free of its ropes underwater, loom up from the lakebed and glide ominously on the surface, the terrible ghost of Christmas past.

Bleak though my mood was on Christmas, the following day lifted my spirits when I noted the distance we had covered in the last twenty-four hours—201 nautical miles! 372 km! The weather may not have brought good cheer, but it did bring good mileage. I was now at the tail end of the second leg of the journey and hope had started to recover its solid, comforting shape again.

On the morning of the 28th, the clocks on the boat had a major tiff. They wouldn't see eye to eye, which in 'clockspeak' meant they told time differently.

The expedition required me to keep track of three time zones: the local time on the boat for my own schedule, Indian Standard Time (IST) for communication with headquarters and Greenwich Mean Time (GMT) or Coordinated Universal Time (UTC) for navigation. To do this, I referred to seven timepieces, adjusting them regularly to the different time zones I passed through. The roll call was as follows:

- A mobile phone clock
- A laptop clock
- A wristwatch
- A digital clock
- A second digital clock
- The GPS time on the electronic chart
- The Inmarsat satellite phone clock

This morning, however, the local clock, the laptop and the wristwatch each struck a different chord and I couldn't tell which of them was lying. What's worse, I had horribly overslept, thanks to ten straight hours of navigation the previous day, and when I woke up—at what the local clock said was 10 a.m.—I realized I was late submitting my morning report . . . which was due at 8! If headquarters did not receive an update from me at the scheduled hour, they would begin to worry. If the update was several hours late, they would start to panic. And if by the end of the day, I was still incommunicado, they would send a search and rescue team to look for me. Luckily, the delay hadn't set off alarm bells yet, and I sent my updates with a thousand apologies.

Now time is paramount if you're running a race like the Vendée Globe. Thankfully, Sagar Parikrama wasn't a race. But even though I wasn't set a deadline, my welcome would be noticeably cold if I took my time returning.

Moreover, I had food rations to last only 200 days. If I ran out, I would have to call in at a port or flag down a passing ship, and that would be the end of the mission. While I wouldn't dream of making port on the sly in an emergency, it *couldn't* be done even if I'd wanted to. Firstly, any foreign boat that lands on the shores of a country will be recorded and reported to the authorities. Secondly, the Inmarsat C—an egg-shaped satellite communications device tacked to the boat—relayed my location every six hours to the Indian Navy.

But most crucial to my timely return was the weather window. The voyage had been planned for winter sailing through the northern hemisphere and summer sailing through the southern hemisphere, to avoid the blistering weather of a southern winter. If I dragged my feet, I would be caught by the worst of the turning seasons.

Apart from these considerations, when you're alone at sea, ungoverned by a stopwatch, what use is time but to know when to say 'hello' to land?

> Time's a burglar. On his toes
> Noiselessly the rascal goes;
> Steals my hair, and in its place
> Drops long wrinkles on my face
> (*Burglar Time* by Amos Russel Wells)

Below the two knuckles of land that make up the beautiful nation of New Zealand—North Island and South Island—are a fistful of smaller isles. These, mapped as five island groups, collectively make up the New Zealand subantarctic islands, strung between 47° and 53° latitude south.

I had now started to climb up from the Furious Fifties and sail north-east, turning a course towards Snares Islands, one of the five in the group. (It got its name from the word 'snare' or 'trap', because its rocks were believed to be hazardous to ships.) It had been fifty-eight days since I had last sighted land, and I was desperate for a glimpse of it, if only to know that life on Earth was as I had left it.

It seemed like it was, because familiar emissaries started flying out to me in the white-bellied, black-backed shape of the Salvin's albatross (named after the English ornithologist Osbert Salvin). They glided around the boat, soaring high, then swooping almost to sea level, signalling that land was only a short flight away.

The New Zealand subantarctic islands are home to an astonishing 126 species of birds! A few centuries ago, however, other uninvited guests started to arrive. They multiplied with such speed that they overran the islands' native species of plants and animals.

The 'foreigners' were goats, pigs and sheep deposited thoughtfully by passing ships as food for castaways and future sailors who dropped anchor there. Even cats were left behind (perhaps for company). Such animal—and even plant—colonization was common practice across remote islands of the world. What the sailors failed to realize then was that the foreigners would in a few short years totally change, and even decimate, the delicate ecosystems of these remote islands.

Although now, in the subantarctic islands at least, all the goats and sheep, cats and cattle, rats and mice that were not native to the islands are being shipped to mainland New Zealand to allow the islands to return to the way they were before the invasion.

(Goats brought to mind the notorious goat on Joshua Slocum's sloop. It ate everything in sight, including his chart of the West Indies. Slocum called it the worst pirate he'd met on the whole voyage! Incidentally, during one of my previous voyages, *that* was the nickname I'd given my crew—Slocum's Goat, because of the way they devoured everything on our boat!)

As for me, I could spot neither sheep nor goat on Snares Islands, because I couldn't spot the islands themselves. A spoilsport wind suddenly sprung up and threw me 33 miles off course. That's a hair's breadth in the life of the ocean! I thought I'd fish in those waters for cod, but despite hours of patiently waiting with my line over the stern, I caught nothing but air, and though it was fresh it would scarcely make a meal.

As I passed the longitude of New Zealand, the sun elbowed the clouds out of the way and beamed down on a new ocean that sparkled with electric blue intensity—the Pacific!

The third leg of the expedition had officially begun.

### The Antipodean Albatross

The Antipodean albatross is only slightly smaller than its cousin, the wandering albatross, which has the greatest wingspan of all birds. It measures from 8-11 ft! So if you stood near a wandering albatross with one outspread wing tip on the ground and the other pointing to the sky, it would tower above the tallest person on Earth.

# Time Travel at the International Date Line

## Third Leg: New Zealand to Cape Horn
## 30 December 2012 to 26 January 2013

It was late September in the year 1513, when a man and his dog reached the summit of a hill, after days of cutting through dense and humid jungle. The man's name was Vasco Núñez de Balboa and his dog was Leoncico.

Behind them walked a long retinue of guides and soldiers, carrying food and tents and everything else vital for comfortable exploration. Before them lay an ocean, piercing blue and dappled gold. The minute he set his squinting eyes upon it, the Spanish explorer earned the honour of becoming the first European to spot the Pacific Ocean. But it wasn't Balboa who gave it this name. He had simply called it *Mar del Sur*, the South Sea.

Seven years after Balboa, *another* European met the ocean. He did not gaze dreamily at it from a hilltop, but sailed right into it on his expedition to the Spice Islands of Indonesia. It was this man, Ferdinand Magellan, who called the ocean *Mar Pacifico*, or Peaceful Sea because that was how tranquil its waters appeared to him.

Whether or not the Pacific was as saintly as Magellan made it out to be was a verdict I would deliver only once I had crossed it. What I knew for now though was, it was the largest and the deepest of the world's five ocean basins. To give their students an idea of just how large and deep this ocean is, geography teachers often say: 'You can tip all the continents of the world into it, and there'd still be room for more.'

It looked exactly like a brilliant, billion-carat sapphire; the best-behaved body of water I had encountered. After the snarling Indian Ocean, the Pacific was singing me a lullaby. I stood on deck and drank in the view. The sullen greys had dissolved into a bright palette of primary colours, and the further east I went, the brighter the skies grew. I was in such good spirits, I decided to treat myself to a packet of biryani pilfered from January's rations. Who was keeping tabs but me, anyway!

At last, the final day of December descended and I launched another round of celebrations. Out came the DFRL halwa and the other half of my Christmas feast, the half-eaten chocolate bar, both of which I swallowed before my teeth knew what had passed through.

I received several New Year emails that day from followers of the mission. One from Admiral D.K. Joshi, the Chief of Naval Staff, read:

*'Your mission continues to be perilous . . . There will be situations that will demand meeting challenges head-on and calculated risks . . . beyond what one encounters in normal life. It is under these circumstances that your years of training and maturity will stand you in good stead and drive you forth to success.'*

The day unfolded smoothly. The sun was warm, the waters lively and the wind generous. *Mhadei*, clipping along at a steady 7 knots, told me to take a break. Grateful for the breather, I settled on the cockpit bunk with my favourite book—*One Hundred Years of Solitude* by Gabriel Garcia Márquez.

A few years ago, when serving on the INS *Delhi*, I remember reading another one of Márquez's books, *The Story of a Shipwrecked Sailor*. Unlike his other novels, there was nothing invented about this story. It described the real-life misadventure of a Columbian sailor who had

been swept off the deck of his naval destroyer in a storm, right into the open waters of the Caribbean Sea.

For ten days, Luis Alejandro Velasco floated on a raft, drifting aimlessly wherever the current took him. Desperately hungry, he chewed whatever he could find—first the business cards in his pocket, then his belt, then his shoes. When one day, a large fish plopped into his frail craft, Luis tore into it with bare teeth. But when he absent-mindedly dunked the fish into the sea to wash the blood off it, a shark reared its arrowhead above the water and snapped the fish whole. The man was lucky to have kept his hand!

Sharks were the constant companion of the castaway, circling his raft every evening at five o'clock, like nuns in a schoolyard. At the end of ten days, just when the sailor was ready to say his final Amen, he caught sight of land and lived to tell his incredible tale. And Marquez, being a journalist at the time, promptly wrote it down.

I'd read so many stories about people at sea, I felt I could see them on the water, and when I did, it transformed the sea from a place without people, to a much-peopled place.

~~~

The year 2012 was now winding to a close and I was inches from the 180th longitude, better known as the International Date Line (IDL). The IDL is a figment of the human imagination, drawn in invisible ink to help us get a grip on time and place. But unlike the others, it's the only longitude that officially divides one calendar date from the next. And it was because of *this* date-deciding meridian that I was able to pull off the greatest time trick of my life! For what I was about to do was travel back to the past . . . but only after I sailed right into the future!

The New Year rolled in and my wristwatch rang the bells. Fireworks went off in my head and I wished *Mhadei* and the ocean the customary greetings. Back in India, which was several longitudes behind me, thanks to the time difference, it was still 5.30 p.m. on 31 December. This meant I had a head start on the New Year. But it was to be curiously short-lived, for, in six short hours, I would return to 31 December of the previous year. Hard to believe?

This is how . . .

The way time-travel works across meridians is that anyone crossing them from west to east—that is, in the direction the earth rotates— earns time. And when they cross the IDL, they earn a whole extra day! So when I stepped across it six hours later, I was smack bang back in 2012, living 31 December all over again. What this meant was I'd be celebrating New Year twice over.

But just because the first New Year had passed without a glitch, didn't mean the second would be its Xerox copy.

I had just dispatched the day's first log and was about to make myself some breakfast, when I decided to turn on the bilge pump first, to pump out the seawater that had collected in the hull. Its engine was deafeningly quiet. This was not good.

The bilge is the hollow, compartmented chamber at the bottom of a boat, running almost the whole length of it.

There are several ways water could fill up a bilge. The most disastrous of these would be if the hull sprang a leak and seawater rushed straight in. That would not only flood the bilge, but could sink the whole boat! Water could also trickle down the mast, which passes right through the bilge and attaches itself to the keel. The keel—also called the backbone of a ship—is the long, narrow wedge running under the hull from bow to stern.

Or water could roll into the cabin from the deck, through the hatch (opening) and down the companionway (passage). In swirling seas, I always double-blocked this hatch with a pair of wooden washboards, mounted one above the other, to keep the water out. Water could also wash in through open portholes. I learnt this the hard way when, through the galley porthole left accidentally open, a rogue wave once spilled into the cabin and soaked the floorboards! When water enters the cabin—as it is bound to on a boat—it simply slips between the planking in the floor and drains into the bilge!

*Mhadei*'s bilge has three compartments. Portioning the water into sections helps to stabilize the vessel, for one vast and heaving volume of it could throw a boat off balance.

If the bilge fills up with water, it could drastically slow down the boat. To avoid this, boats are fitted with bilge pumps that have to simply be switched on for the water to be spat back into the sea. Only my pump couldn't do its job, because it was broken! I tried switching it on several times, but it was dead as driftwood. Muttering several unprintable words, I prepared to nosedive into the repairs.

Now, what's that they say about a great ship asking for deep waters?

As if one end-of-year calamity wasn't enough, the fates chose to double my trouble. The raw-water pump of the electricity generator stopped working too! This pump draws in seawater to cool the generator's little engine. But sometimes, the pump draws air instead, and that can make it can heat up and crack. Without the pump, the generator itself wouldn't work and we know what would happen then! (All the electrical devices would shut down.) It was the second time the generator had gone out of order. So now I needed to fix two pumps!

Contrary to what people imagine, a solo circumnavigation isn't simply a matter of trimming sails and taking photographs. It means being able to solve any problem the ocean throws at you. And just like I couldn't pull into a port for food if I ran out of rations, I couldn't pull into a port for repairs if something seized up. I ought to know how to fix everything myself, from a broken bone to a broken engine.

And because my training before the expedition included electrical repairs, I knew just what to do.

Leaping into action, I rummaged in the stores for spares and finding what I wanted, set about fixing both machines. After about half an hour with the toolkit—keeping my tongue firmly in check for fear of aggravating the pumps with my curses—I managed to resuscitate both and get them whirring back to life.

## Women in Sailing

Almost until the nineteenth century, sailing was out of bounds for women. It wasn't only believed to be bad form to have women on board, but bad luck as well!

And yet, some of them were so determined to sail, they slipped into all-men crews disguised as men! They wore trousers and jackets, cut their hair short and stained their faces with grease and dirt to go unnoticed. Some managed to go far with their camouflage.

In 1766, a Frenchwoman named Jeanne Baret joined the crew of the Étoile on a round-the-world plant-hunting expedition. She's considered the first woman to circumnavigate the globe! It is believed that the riotous bougainvillaea was discovered by Baret on this expedition. But the plant was named after the commander, Louis Antoine de Bougainville. Baret went undetected for over a year with the help of her lover, a botanist, whom she assisted. But when she was discovered, it is believed her own crew attacked her.

Often, the women had male co-conspirators who helped keep their secret. From the nineteenth century onwards, more women made it to the decks, but largely as passengers. In a few cases, women even helped run the ship, but only when their husbands were captains.

It was late evening by the time I stowed the tools away and finished the run of the boat's chores. Time now for the last meal of 2012. I decided to start with a hot mug of malt to warm me up. Placing water to boil on the gimballed burner, I was just about to scoop out the powdered milk, when without a word of warning, the boat lurched violently, kicked in the side by a mean-minded wave! I was thrown clean over to the leeward side (opposite the wind-hit side), the scalding water from the saucepan spilling over me. Thankfully, the several layers of winter clothing I had on protected me from what would have been a memorable burn.

I fervently prayed no further mishap should visit me before the day was out, and when at midnight 2013 arrived the second time round, I heaved a sigh of relief and made my first New Year's resolution: never resurrect a dead year!

# View from the Top of the Mast

The first day of 2013 blew me away. Literally.

With winds gusting at 52 knots (over 96 km/hour), the sails could have easily taken wing and flown the boat off into the sky like a storm petrel. But *Mhadei* stood her ground and gripped the waters with her talons.

**Motion, motion everywhere and not a spot that's still.**

What's worse than a sailboat stuck on static seas? A sailboat tossed about like a shuttlecock. What's worse than being tossed about like a shuttlecock? Going half-deaf in the bargain. For the racket was *tremendous . . .* and unceasing. The wind howled and the waves crashed into each other and the boat. The effect was enough to crack the strongest eardrums, if not the stoutest nerves. I knew of sailors who wore earplugs and even helmets to keep themselves from going deaf (or mad!). But I've lived in Indian cities that are far more raucous, so I was able to withstand the din.

A few days after the gale, however, the wind pulled in the reins and all stood still. I was held fast, like a toy boat in a bathtub.

Since I couldn't wrench the wind from the sky, I had no choice but to wait out the dead time. Although this wasn't a race to the finish line, I had hoped to complete the journey in six to eight months, taking into account damage to sails, bad weather and still waters. By my estimate, I ought to have finished the Pacific run in forty days. 'But if the wind continues to drag its feet like this, I'll be here to ring in another New Year,' I said to myself unhappily. Thankfully, the weather isn't set in stone. Three days later, the winds picked up and I was on my way around the world again.

~~~

On 9 January 2013, I broke the first record of the expedition! I crossed the 10,000-mile mark to become the first Indian to sail that distance alone, without stopping! Back home, much would have been made of this. Fireworks would have been set off by my family, and sweets distributed to half the city. Indians celebrate all great accomplishments with something sweet. An exam passed. A medal won. A door unstuck. A ladoo. A peda. A jalebi. It was no wonder every other shop in the country was a sweet shop.

Keeping with custom, I carried my own stash of sweets. Only, instead of a sticky jalebi, I drew out a bar of strawberry-flavoured freeze-dried ice cream—a gift from Aneesh, sent all the way from New Zealand to India, to be eaten on some happy day in the South Pacific.

On the morning of 11 January, I woke up and stretched as much as the narrow bunk would allow me. I was in good spirits. Having had an excellent night's sleep—a bumper crop of four straight hours—I was raring to begin the day. Little did I know that before the morning passed, I'd be stretched out once more. Only this time, not horizontally and at sea level, but vertically and up in the air— 80 ft above my very bunk!

I took my malt out on the deck and walked around the boat on my usual inspection. That's when I noticed something odd. One of the lazy jacks of the stack pack had come loose. Lazy jacks are lines or ropes on either side of the mainsail. They run from somewhere near the top of the mast all the way to the stack pack below, on the boom—the horizontal pole that sticks out from the bottom of the mast. The stack

pack is a canvas container running lengthwise along the boom. Lazy jacks hold the stack pack up so that when I reef or lower the mainsail, it folds down neatly into it. Without the stack pack to contain it, the heavy mainsail would flop all over the deck and I'd have to spend hours fastening it to the boom.

I now spotted one of these lines trailing in the water. I moaned in exasperation. This meant work. Then I saw *another* problem. The main line holding up the stack pack had been pulled right up to the second spreader on the mast. Spreaders are spars or short poles that angle out in pairs on either side of the mast to support it. I knew with a sinking heart what I had to do—reattach the runaway line to the mast. This meant much more work! And the only way to do it was to climb the 69-foot mast itself.

I had climbed *Mhadei*'s mast before, but only when she was docked and stationary! The only time I'd climbed a mast in the open ocean was when we had to hoist the Sri Lankan flag when sailing to Sri Lanka. But we were a whole crew back then, and going up the mast was really a matter of stepping into a harness and being winched up by the other sailors, like a pot of water raised from a well.

Not so easy when you're both pot and person pulling it!

Sailors who find themselves in such a wrenching situation rely on mountaineering equipment specially modified for yachts. Now given a chance, most single-handers choose *when* to scale a mast. They wait for the perfect day when just the right amount of wind meets just the right amount of swell to hold the boat steady.

I, on the other hand, had to get the job done immediately, for, in a few short hours, I knew the frenzied south-westerlies would come knocking.

Cracking my knuckles, I drew a deep breath and headed down to brush my teeth. That done, I gulped down an energy drink and changed into a

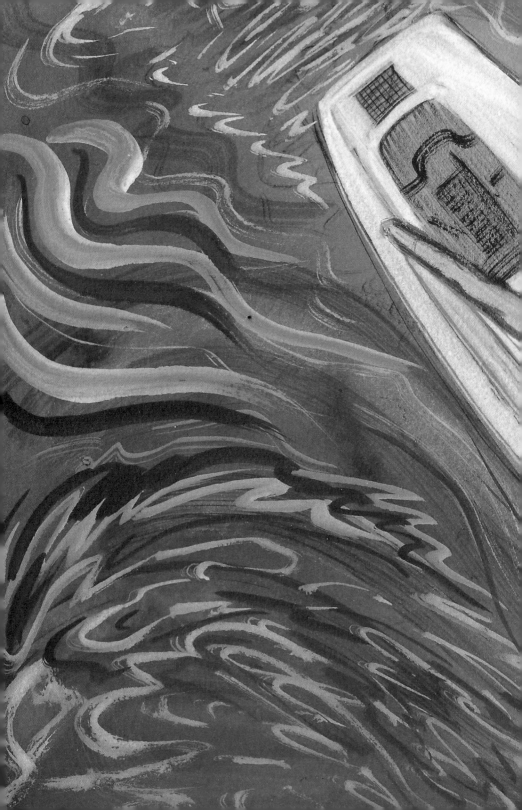

clean set of clothes. I shed my heavy layers so that I'd have less of myself to hoist up the rope. I then fixed the camera to the deck to film my climb.

When the mast-climbing gear had arrived from Europe, I prayed I'd never have to put its advertised features to the test. But the prayer, like the lazy jack, had gone adrift. Cursing my luck, I started to rig the climbing lines. I strapped the yellow harness between my legs and around my waist, and fastened the buckles, consulting the instruction manual as I went. In ten minutes, I was all strapped in and seated in the bosun's chair, the small planked bench that's part of the mast-climbing equipment. And so, harnessed and in the hot seat, I started to lift off the ground in slow and unsteady flight.

The promotional video for the mast-climber made the exercise look easier than climbing into bed. It wasn't. It was more like climbing up a pole twice the height of a lamp post, with a 4-metre swell underfoot, and a bouncing wind overhead. Because that's exactly what it was.

With hands and feet gripping the rope, I swung wildly in the air, the wind pawing me like a cat swiping at a feather. I oscillated from left to right of the mast, each time slamming midway with a mighty thump straight into its cold hard metal.

Luckily, neither mast nor bones broke and I inched up slowly. After suffering a few more murderous thwacks, I found a way to sidestep the blows. Every time I sensed the wind picking up, I braced myself by reaching out with one hand for a nearby halyard and sticking my feet forward to avoid slamming into the mast. And in the few seconds the wind paused to catch its breath, I'd scramble up another foot. It was slow and excruciating work, but finally, after about sixty muscle-mincing minutes, I made it up to the second spreader, 12 m above the deck. It was slightly colder at that height than it was on deck below, and I felt the boat's rolling motion more keenly. I tied a knot on the rope to keep my harness from slipping back down and proceeded to untangle the lines.

When finally the job was done, I paused to take in the view.

Spread out before me was the unending ocean. Equal in its blue-greyness, unbroken in its breadth, neither craft nor creature split its surface. Like a primordial being it slept, heaving and sighing and all the while cradling the origins of life in its lap.

On that day at that perch, I knew it wasn't blood, but the ocean that ran through my veins.

## India's First All-Women Circumnavigation

Four years after Abhilash Tomy returned from his circumnavigation, six Indian women set out on theirs. On 10 September 2017, the six—all officers with the Indian Navy—sailed the INSV *Tarini* on what would become India's first all-women circumnavigation under sail. The expedition was called Navika Sagar Parikrama. 'Navika', which in Sanskrit means 'new', also contains the Sanskrit word for 'ship'—'nav'.

The INSV *Tarini* was skippered by Lieutenant Commander Vartika Joshi, with Lieutenant Commanders Pratibha Jamwal, P. Swathi and Lieutenants Vijaya Devi, Aishwarya Boddapati and Payal Gupta as crew. They had been coached by Captain Dilip Donde.

The women made themselves at home on the boat. Apart from navigating, trimming sails, fixing and mending things that came apart, they watched films, listened to music and celebrated birthdays with balloons and freshly baked cakes. Incidentally, the crew had trained on *Mhadei* before embarking on the *Tarini*, a 55-foot vessel built at the same shipyard as the *Mhadei*.

After eight months and 21,600 nautical miles at sea—dropping anchor at five ports on the way—the sailors returned home on 21 May 2018, with a new record to their names.

# A Trip to the Bottom of the Ocean

A thought sometimes struck me as I floated there, on the skin of the sea: *What if some intergalactic prankster pulled a plug in the planet and drained every last drop of Earth's water into its red-hot core? All 1.3 billion cubic km of it?*

I'd eddy down in a whirlpool to the ocean floor, an aquanaut out of aqua. And there, plain as the glaciers and rainforests above the sea, I'd discover what was hidden *beneath* it. Without its cloak of water, the seabed would reveal itself, one distinctive landform after the other: ridges and ravines, hills and valleys, plateaus and plains, mountains, and even riverbeds!

At the bottom, I'd trek across abyssal plains brown and flat as cakes, until I'd arrive at the Ring of Fire, the circle of marine volcanoes in the Pacific basin. But I'd hurry on out of there, because 70 per cent of all volcanic eruptions on Earth take place underwater! Elsewhere on the seabed, I'd spot seamounts and guyots—underwater tabletop mountains. The Pacific has more of these than any other ocean basin (196 out of Earth's 283).

After weeks of walking, I'd eventually land up at the base of a ridge, those jagged chains of submarine mountains that unspool into kilometre-long ranges. It's funny how humans gaze up gobsmacked at the Himalayas and the Andes, those spectacular steeples above sea level, when all the while the real leviathans lurk underwater! If the length of all the mountain ridges in the five ocean basins was totalled,

it would add up to over 80,000 km! Mountain climbers would be over the moon.

But if there was one ocean feature I'd give my left eye to see, it would have to be the Mariana Trench in the western Pacific basin, a crescent-shaped gash 2550 km long and 69 km wide. Trenches are deep cuts in the crust where the ground plunges thousands of metres as if cloven with a long axe. They're formed by the collision of tectonic plates, when one plate is pushed under the other, into the mantle of the earth itself.

It is in the blackest depths of the Mariana Trench that the deepest point on Earth resides—the Challenger Deep. If Mount Everest itself were to be dropped into this dark dungeon, its peak would still be 1.6 km beneath the water's surface.

As I stood at the lip of the trough, picturing the mountain within the canyon like a finger within a fist, another image assembled before my mind—a dream within a dream. This time, all the seamounts, guyots and ridges were razed to the ground. Deep gouges scored the ocean floor like empty eye sockets, and here and there were raw gashes, as though a terrible demon had raked the earth.

Mining machines!

They had done to the ocean floor what they did to the ground above— scoured it for minerals and metals. For after they'd dug up all the minerals on dry land, they'd begun to mine the seabed, killing sea life as they went. Even as I watched, horrified, a heavy cloud of sediment lifted off the clawed earth and drew near.

Floating within it were dead plankton and the carcasses of sea cucumbers and sawn-off tube worms. The brown cloud was now inches from my nose and about to swallow me like it had the rest . . . when I felt something land on my head. A raindrop. Then another and another. What started as a drizzle turned into a full-blown downpour! It rained and rained until the deadly cloud dispersed, and the ocean basins started to fill up again. In a matter of minutes, they were full to the brim, and I found myself in my boat on the water's back, leaving the ocean floor as it was when I first met it. And its grim future where I hoped *never* to meet it.

Having returned from the exploration in my head, I turned my attention to the expedition at hand. Strangely enough, I found myself at a spot on the ocean as surreal as everything below it. The remotest place on Planet Earth . . . a spot so removed from habitation that the nearest humans were probably the astronauts in the International Space Station overhead!

Point Nemo.

Located at 48°52.6'S 123°23.6'W—around the intersection of the 48th latitude south and the 123rd longitude west—Point Nemo is 1458 nautical miles from land. A place so far away, it's called the 'Oceanic Pole of Inaccessibility'.

It has another, creepier title: 'Spacecraft Cemetery'! Because it's so far from inhabited parts of the planet—and virtually undisturbed by passing ships—this is the defenceless black hole space scientists have chosen to have spacecraft and satellite debris fall back to Earth. Only 4 km below me was that watery wasteland of fragmented satellites and spent fuel tanks that not long ago orbited the planet. The odds of a chunk of solid satellite hitting a human being in these parts was 1:10,000. Let me not be *that* one, I frantically prayed.

And yet for all its great distance, Point Nemo is closer to India than to any other place on earth. At least in the literary sense! After all, the spot is named after Captain Nemo, the deep-sea adventurer of the Jules Verne classic *Twenty Thousand Leagues Under the Sea*.

And Nemo happens to be the son of a raja from Bundelkhand—a region in and of India!

By now, I had been at sea for seventy-seven days, and my ears were ringing. There's never a quiet moment on the water. Even at its calmest, the ocean murmurs. As the waves rub shoulders, they make a steady whooshing sound, like sand sliding up and down the wooden hollow of a rain stick. Closer to the boat, they lap against the hull like a thousand cats slurping milk all at once, gulping loudly now and then.

In rough weather, the sounds are entirely different. The waves crash like whole forests felled! Worst of all is the sound of angry waves slapping the boat. One cubic metre of water weighs one ton. Now imagine a wave 8 m high and 20 m wide giving the boat a sound slap!

Then there's the wind. It goes from a low whistle to a high keening as it picks up speed, sounding like a bunch of sickly sirens. Streaking through the sails, it makes a *thwacking* sound as it jerks the broad, heavy cloth. And as it puts its great weight on the ropes and rigging, straining and bullying, it makes them creak like bending wood. To hear this is to imagine, petrified, that the boat is about to crack at the seams.

The cabin likewise is no quiet chapel. As the boat rolls from side to side, things roll around with it, making uncountable tiny noises: tools, cutlery and spares giving out little clinks and rattles that grow louder and sharper with the pitching of the sea.

Now, my ears may have been bruised, but there was nothing wrong with my nose. One day despite the brisk breeze, I began to detect an awful odour, similar to ripening compost. For long seconds, I puzzled over it. And then I realized, it was *I* who was that rotting heap! The reason was quite simple, really—it had been two weeks since my last bucket bath. But despite the stink I raised, I wasn't about to repeat the nightmare of bathing straight from the ocean. The water was 6°C, cold enough to freeze my bones and turn my quaking teeth into ice cubes. Not until I reached warmer waters a month later would I pull up another pail for a bath, I vowed. Not even if I reeked like a rotter till then.

But why was I hauling buckets of seawater for a bath in that frigid weather in the first place? Why was I not showering in the comfort of my tiny bath cubicle? Because the boat's water maker had gone kaput! Dead. Demised. Deceased.

It happened two weeks ago when I noticed with a small pang of panic that neither taps nor showerhead sprang freshwater. The reason for this was the lifeless water maker. This prodigious device converted salty seawater into (tolerable) freshwater, which was then stored in the water tanks under the floorboards. All the taps on board drew on these tanks for their supply. Without the water maker, I might as well have hauled up buckets straight out of the sea.

At first, I fetched my toolkit and tried to fix the device. But no amount of probing or picking could get it to work. After a couple of hours, I gave up in frustration. The consequence of this new conundrum was not so much my limited supply of freshwater for bathing, but my finite reserves for drinking! For even though I drank from the packaged bottles, the water tanks were my fallback.

I had to now ration the 400 litres of potable water available on the boat to last until the end of the expedition. If everything went according to plan and I made steady progress, I would have 4.5 litres a day to see me through the next three months until l reached home. This may seem more than enough to anyone sitting under a ceiling fan in an armchair at home. But a solo circumnavigator spends *vast* reserves of energy doing the sundry and super-exhausting things such a voyage demands and needs to stay hydrated all the time.

I didn't need much water in cold weather, but as the weather warmed (as it soon would), I knew I'd start to sweat copiously as I went about fixing lines and sails under the glaring sun. The cabin too would begin to warm up like a brick.

Of course, there were always things one could do. To conserve water, some sailors control their thirst by eating foods with little salt. Some cut back on the water they drink. They bathe when it rains and harvest the rain. And some use seawater for everything—from brushing their teeth to bathing, to cooking a meal and washing the dishes.

Now that I had no steady supply of freshwater, I adopted a few of these water-saving measures myself. I rinsed most of the dirty utensils in seawater. When I did use freshwater to rinse a plate out, I drank the greasy water instead of draining it, swallowing bits of leftover gravy and vegetables with it.

The broken machine may have forced me to be tight-fisted with the water, but it also gave me bragging rights. I could now say without lying that I had bathed in the waters of the Indian Ocean, the Pacific *and* the Atlantic (on a previous journey). But to avoid jinxing myself, I decided to gloat only *after* I had safely dropped anchor in India.

Until then, I had to go about the hair-splitting business of running a one-man crew single-handedly—sailing as captain, handyman, cook and deckhand, all rolled into one.

In fickle winds that changed direction within the hour, it was Deckhand Abhilash who adjusted the sheets or ropes. In the obstacle course of the southern Indian Ocean, it was Helmsman Abhilash who steered the boat clear of growlers. On calm seas, it was Deckhand Abhilash who mended sails ripped by wind or weathering. Abhilash the Chef rustled up a meal of mashed potato when the weather was good enough to cook, while Record Keeper Abhilash took photographs and wrote blogs, documenting the expedition as it unfolded. It was

Communications Officer Abhilash who sent and received dispatches from land, and Chaplain Abhilash who sent up hectic prayers when a storm blew up. And in command of it all was Captain Abhilash, who made sure neither crew nor vessel buckled under the enormous strain of sailing alone around the world.

## The Challenger Expedition

Until the mid-nineteenth century, people knew very little about what lay within the ocean. On 7 December 1872, a small wooden warship set off to find out. The HMS Challenger left Portsmouth, England, with two British naturalists at the helm to unearth the ocean's secrets. With laboratories and complex scientific equipment, it travelled for three and a half years across the world, recording the water's depth and temperature, and collecting samples of rock and marine life from different parts of the ocean. By the time it returned to Britain on 26 May 1876, it had collected over 4000 new species of plants and animals, along with maps it had drawn of the ocean floors. Modern oceanography had just begun.

# Mammoths Attack

I knuckled my eyes wearily, trying to grind down the slabs of sleep that lay over each eye like a tombstone. The previous day, on 20 January, a Force 10 storm rose and knocked the wind clean out of me. Waves drove in over the horizon, grey and immense like a herd of woolly mammoths. Fifty-foot pounders, they smashed into *Mhadei*, bent on scuppering the boat. For over twenty straight hours, they kept coming and for nearly all of those hours, I was on my feet. Or to be accurate, on my hands *and* feet, for I sometimes had to crawl around on the deck on all fours to keep myself from losing balance and toppling over.

I was no steadier inside the cabin. Moving around the tiny space required me to stretch out my arms like a scaffold, reaching for walls and grab handles to stay upright as the boat rolled. The rolling and pitching had me tossing about from port to starboard, and with every lurch, I slammed hard against something or other, the air rushing out of my lungs like steam from a piston. *Mhadei* heeled or went sideways time and time again, leaning closer and closer to the water at dangerous angles. Each time she tilted, I was sure she was going to capsize, but she always found her feet again.

At times like this, the safest place is inside the cabin. Scores of sailors have been snapped up by the sea when out on deck in similar weather. Some were sucked in by a ravenous wave. Others slipped across water-slick planks and bounced over the gunwale when their boat suddenly heeled. On older, square-rigged ships, with sails stacked along the yardarms (the horizontal poles on a mast, at right angles to it), sailors have even been plucked clean off the ropes or rigging if they had the

misfortune to be up there in a gale, untangling the lines or securing loose sails.

I'd read about single-handers like myself, whose boats had capsized in storms. One found himself on the ceiling of his cabin when his boat turned turtle. He managed to climb out through the escape hatch, to be finally rescued by a search vessel two whole days later.

Another sailor's ketch, or two-masted sailboat, rolled 360° like a log. It righted itself again, but not before water sluiced into the cabin through a broken porthole, flooding it. Yet another sailor lost a finger to a hatch that slammed shut in the tumult. In such times, it's not just the courage and resilience of sailors that are put to the test, but their skills at navigation, their knowledge of the boat, and their ability to think fast on their feet even as their feet hit the ceiling.

Sodden, chilled and rattled to the bone, I waited out the turbulent weather. The storm would pass, I knew. And after what seemed like unending hours, the wind did pipe down and the seas settled. By now, it was ten in the morning. After a quick scan of the weather forecast to make sure another storm wasn't about to sneak up on me, I battened down the cabin hatch and fell like lead into my bed.

Sailors going alone on long and dangerous voyages don't sleep like folks on land. They might get as much as six hours or as little as fifteen minutes of sleep in one whole day—but *only* when the weather lets them go to bed at all. Days it doesn't, a sailor might be awake for a full twenty-four or even forty-eight hours, battling the elements. And that can be very, very dangerous. Because when sailors don't get sufficient sleep, they're not well rested. And when they're not well rested, all kinds of nasty things can happen. They start to lose their memory, they find it hard to concentrate, they make wrong decisions while navigating, they become irritable and anxious, and worst of all—they hallucinate!

Now, it's one thing to occasionally daydream while you're staring out at a quiet sea. But if sailors are not careful to get the rest they need, they might mix up the world within them for the world around them. Some sleep-deprived sailors drifting for long days in troubling weather imagine they've arrived home already, picturing crowds of people cheering them at the harbour—when they are, in fact, still in the middle of the ocean! It is even said of some that they imagine they've moored their boat at a wharf and start to climb out on to an unseen quay, only to sink straight into the sea.

As for me, I was careful to rest every chance I got. In good weather, I managed to sleep six hours a day, and in bad weather, no more than four—not at a stretch, but in fitful snatches of an hour or two at a time. We call this pattern of choppy sleep, 'polyphasic sleep'. In my kind of sleep, dreams came quickly and when they did, they were a special kind of virtual reality.

~~~

Out of the far sky on the horizon, a speck materialized. As it drew near, it slowly resolved into the shape of a dinghy. Then, into the shape of a man in a dinghy. The wooden vessel looked like it had weathered a thousand storms. The man, a million. He was gaunt and miserable, his beard and hair were moonlight white and his face, a suntanned shade of apricot. Deep crevasses fanned out from his eyes which were hard as tamarind seeds. Each skeletal hand wrapped loosely around an oar that he rhythmically rotated through the water.

'Magellan?' I asked, uncertainly. Something told me this ragged spectre was that legendary sailor who'd circumnavigated the globe.

My own predecessor, in a sense.

The man glared up at me. 'What?' he snarled.

'What an honour it is, Magellan . . . Sir . . . to meet the world's first circumnavigator!' I gushed, sounding a bit silly even to myself. 'I'm circumnavigating too. Only I'm going east to west, in the opposite direction you'd travelled. Any advice you'd like to give me? You know, good counsel, tried-and-tested tips, word to the wise, that sort of thing?'

'Go back,' he spat. 'Don't do it. Cease and desist. Stop and return. That sort of thing.'

'What!' I exclaimed.

'I attempted that madcap mission and look where I landed! My crew mutinied—not once, but twice; we nearly ran out of food; we set out with five ships and only one returned . . . and if that doesn't dissuade you, I was speared to death on the expedition itself!'

'But,' I protested, 'it's because of *that* pioneering journey that you're still famous 500 years later. You're on stamps, banknotes, T-shirts . . . even on a bottle of gin!'

'Burn them all!' he growled. 'First of all, you know that's not true. I *did not* complete the circumnavigation. Did I return to the starting point? I only made it three-quarters of the way. So what if you all remember me now? I'd have much preferred riches in life, thank you very much. Now go back home and take up a safer profession . . . like baking,' he muttered and started rowing away.

That, unfortunately, was the fate of many sailors—to endlessly skim the seas, angry and bitter, with not a kind word to dispense. I had yet to meet a ghost in good spirits.

I woke up with a start. Shaking my head free of the fading *plunk* of Magellan's oars, I headed up to the deck. Nothing but grey sky and grey water. It was 2 a.m. on 26 January. An early summer morning in the southern hemisphere. Even at this hour, there was a lingering purple light in the sky. I thought of Lewis Carroll.

The sun was shining on the sea,

Shining with all his might:

He did his very best to make

The billows smooth and bright—

And this was odd because it was

The middle of the night.

*(Through the Looking-Glass)*

Although my eye could not yet cast a line out to it, there, just beyond the ashy horizon lay Cape Horn, the milestone that would mark the beginning of the end of Sagar Parikrama II. Some call Cape Horn the 'Everest of Oceans' because the foaming waters around it are as dangerous and deadly as the icy slopes of the mountain.

Cape Horn is the southernmost point of a knot of islands in Chile called Tierra del Fuego, the Land of Fire. At 56° south, it is also the southernmost of the three Great Capes, of which I had already rounded Leeuwin. Good Hope was still waiting down the road.

Although it looks no more sinister than a dark lump of land fronted by a few pillars of rock, hundreds of sailors have been gored by the Horn. They've drowned in the choppy waters surrounding it or been dragged by the strong current and dashed against the rocks. Gales and screaming winds stir up the seas here, raising white-veined waves tall as pine trees. This place too is called the graveyard of sailors.

To cross this thorny outcrop, I had to plunge into the Drake Passage, a 540 km-wide corridor of icy water named after Sir Francis Drake, the sixteenth-century English admiral and circumnavigator. Wind

and water blow and flow from west to east in the Drake Passage and help form a loop of current called the Antarctic Circumpolar Current, the strongest ocean current on Earth that winds all the way around Antarctica. It was to this very current that I had now hitched a ride.

In the months leading up to the expedition, I had taken a measuring tape to the voyage, to know *when* I would reach a certain point in the journey if everything went to plan. By my estimate, I had hoped to cross The Horn on India's Republic Day, 26 January. It had never before been celebrated in this corner of the planet before.

To my good luck, weather and water played along. And so it was that at 3.15 a.m. on the deck clock and 1.45 p.m. in India, I found myself celebrating India's Republic Day 17 nautical miles south of Cape Horn and 8100 nautical miles from home. Fetching up the Indian national flag from the hold, I hoisted it on the boat's backstay. And there, the orange, white and green rectangle carved a cheerful window in the grey wall of sea and sky.

In that remotest wilderness, with the flag flapping hysterically in the wind, I saluted and sang the national anthem, 'Jana Gana Mana'. My only audience was the population of those parts, a pod of synchronized dolphins and a fly-past of cormorants and albatrosses.

Then, after eighty-six long days at sea, I made four calls to India on the satellite phone. The first was to my parents in Kerala, who were celebrating their thirty-fifth wedding anniversary that day. The second was to Admiral Awati, the man who set me on this course. The third was to Captain Dilip Donde, my mentor. And the last was to Ratnakar Dandekar, the builder of the boat. I congratulated them in turn, because the achievement was equally theirs as it was mine. The admiral had written a poem for the occasion, and he read it out to me on the phone.

*On the day we proclaimed a republic, good and free*

*Twenty-sixth of January two thousand one three*

Mhadei *and Man will pass the Horn*

*Many a gallant sailor's nemesis and thorn*

*And show the flag to the rock and albatross*

Naturally, lunch on that eventful day had to be another mega meal. The rounding of Cape Horn was a big deal because it took three parts skill and seven parts luck to cross it. And the latter, in these parts, was a slippery thing.

I extracted a packet each of DFRL's biryani and kheer from the food rations, and settling down on the cockpit bunk, ate hungrily as I gazed at the Horn wrapped in a cottony cocoon of mist.

Now, I hadn't come all this way only to slip quietly past this storied cape without getting a closer look at it. My navigational screen told me the Horn was near, but I couldn't penetrate its cover. Deciding to venture nearer I gybed, or changed course with the wind behind me, and made it to within 1 nautical mile of Hornos, the island on which the cape is pinned. To my tremendous luck, the fog thinned out *just then* and *just enough* to allow me to take in the Horn's hazy outline as it sat there, cold and forbidding.

But suddenly, as if furious at me for staring, the Horn decided to teach me a lesson in manners. A punishing wind struck up and within long seconds, flew into a rage that whipped the boat with stinging gusts. It lashed and lashed at us in such a fit that I was afraid it would rip the sails to ribbons, but all it took was a foot of foresail from the bottom of the genoa. Unsatisfied with the measly bit of fabric, it then set its sights on the camera I had mounted on the roof of the cabin. Lassoing

it with the mainsheet—the rope that controls the mainsail—the wind wrenched it from its perch, where I thought I had secured it well, and flung it wide into the sea.

'Show's over, pal,' I heard the Horn hiss. 'If you want to make the finish line, you'd better get a move on.' So I hurriedly did.

The Horn had extracted its toll in a camera and a strip of sail. But it had, whether with a closed or open fist, given *me* something too—the matchless title of 'Cape Horner', bestowed on all those who managed to get past it alive. As sailing tradition went, the title came with two badges of honour—one was the gold loop I could now proudly wear on my left ear (the ear that faced the Horn in my west-to-east passage) and the second was the license to forever plant one leg loftily on any table at mealtimes. What's more, in a couple of months, I hoped to earn the double distinction of rounding both capes, Horn *and* Good Hope. And those who won this double dare were within their right to fix *both* feet on the table at every meal. (Until, that is, their mothers or admirals walked into the room.)

## Ferdinand Magellan

Ferdinand Magellan was the first sailor to sail around the world, right? Wrong! While he did set off from Spain on 20 September 1519, with five ships, it was his fellow navigator, Juan Sebastián del Cano, who completed the expedition. Magellan himself was killed in battle on the island of Mactan in the Philippines on 27 April 1521, leaving del Cano to return to Spain on 6 September 1522, with one ship, the Vittoria. Technically, it was del Cano who completed the world's first known circumnavigation! But it was Ferdinand's daring and conviction—that a western sea route to the Spice Islands (Moluccas in Indonesia) existed—that paved a new sea path from west to east.

# Out of the Blue

## Fourth Leg: Cape Horn to Cape of Good Hope
## 27 January 2013 to 19 February 2013

On the morning of my eighty-eighth day at sea, *Mhadei* glided by a low island. My charts identified the place as Isla de Los Estados. It belonged to Argentina, whose mainland lay close, to the west. The name caught on the hook of an old memory. Where had I read about it before? Then suddenly it struck me! The lighthouse on this island was the very same one that had inspired Jules Verne's book, *The Lighthouse at the End of the World*! I rushed into the cabin and pulled out my binoculars.

As the boat sailed past it, I eagerly scoured the island for the famous lighthouse, whose actual name was Faro San Juan de Salvamento. But I spotted neither light nor house. I shrugged. Well at least it was land, and unlike the Horn, it had shown itself to me without making me pay a hefty price.

Now here's something incredible. Even as I searched vainly for signs of life in front of me, they lay right *behind* me all that time! When I turned my back on the island disappointedly, I noticed astern of my boat the spire of a mast, shooting up like a roving telephone pole. Another boat! A yacht! I couldn't believe it. I had grown so accustomed to having birds and fish for company, I wasn't quite sure what to say to another human being, for surely there was life within that wandering vessel and I ought to say hello to it.

I rushed down into the cabin to check the automatic identification system (AIS) on the electronic chart display. This is a tracking system that gives boats at sea crucial information about other boats within a certain range—20 nautical miles in my case. Information like the name of the vessel, its position in latitude and longitude, the speed at which it is travelling, the course it is taking and the point and time at which it is likely to come nearest one's own vessel.

The yacht appeared to be half a nautical mile away. *Erica XII*, it said on the display panel. I grabbed the black handset of the very high frequency (VHF) radio and spoke tentatively into it:

'*Erica XII*, *Erica XII*, this is the INSV *Mhadei*.'

A brief electric crackle, and then . . .

'INSV *Mhadei*, this is *Erica XII*.'

It was the voice of a woman. I realized with a small jolt that the last woman I'd spoken to was my mother.

'You're the first boat I've seen in nearly three months,' I said with the delighted relief one feels on spotting a friend in a crowd.

'Why, where are you sailing from?'

'From Mumbai, in India. I'm on a non-stop single-handed circumnavigation.'

'Wow! That's incredible,' the woman said.

'What about you? Where are you headed?' I asked. I realized after months of chatting silently with fictional friends, I had to make a small effort to draw out spoken words, as if they were at the bottom of a deep well.

'We've sailed out from Ushuaia, and are heading to Antarctica for research,' the woman replied.

Ushuaia, a town in the Tierra del Fuego archipelago, is incidentally called the 'End of the World'. And here was *Erica XII*, I thought, going over its edge.

We exchanged a few more pleasantries and then with 'good luck and goodbye', wished each other fair winds and continued on our separate ways. Strangely, no sooner had *Erica XII* fallen over the horizon, I felt more alone than before I'd met her. Then I thought of Bernard Moitessier and wondered if I'd ever have the nerve to do what *he* had done.

## Bernard Moitessier

Born in Saigon, Vietnam in 1925, Bernard Moitessier decided early on he preferred the ocean to land, and crossed it in boats he built himself. In 1963, he and his wife, Françoise, sailed his yacht, Joshua (named after Joshua Slocum) all the way from France to Tahiti, without stopping.

When the Golden Globe Race was announced in 1968—the first solo, non-stop race across the globe—everyone expected Bernard to win. But when he rounded Cape Horn, the Frenchman decided to go wherever the wind led him. If it blew north, up the Atlantic, he would go ahead and complete the race. And if the wind blew east, he would continue sailing around the world again. The wind blew east, and Bernard just kept on sailing to Tahiti, circumnavigating the globe not once, but just shy of twice!

# A Familiar Bird Flies in

A long time ago, there existed a large island. Around it sprang several smaller islands in concentric circles until the whole archipelago resembled a giant bullseye.

Taken together, the islands were the most spectacular anyone had ever seen. Their trees hung with fruit so large and glossy they seemed artificial. And from their springs sprang water so sparkling it could be bottled and sold at the price of wine. Atlas was the name of the islands' part-god part-mortal king, while his kingdom, part-land part-water was called Atlantis.

Atlantis was a modern and inventive place, full of bold and clever people. They built a racetrack for horses, public fountains with hot *and* cold water, and on the very central island, a silver-plated temple to their father-God, Poseidon.

They were initially a good lot, these Atlanteans. Wise, hard-working and prosperous, they would have been the envy of the world . . . but for one thing. They started to grow hungry for power and wealth. As their hunger grew, so did their snaky schemes and perfidious plots. Angered by their arrogance and lust, the gods devised the ultimate punishment for them. They commanded the ocean to open wide and swallow Atlantis whole. And that is exactly what happened. When the waters closed over the city, it was as if it hadn't existed at all! Atlantis would never be seen again, only remembered until memory lasts, as the Lost City.

The only part of Atlantis that continues to survive is the tub of water that once kept it afloat—the Atlantic Ocean. The one I was currently crossing.

Only an ocean away from home, *Mhadei* skimmed the water, her sails singing. The sun was out and basking on the foredeck in its runny 10°C warmth, I too was in high spirits. At times like this, I was happy to be heading home . . . happy I was halfway through the expedition.

*Mhadei* and I were making good time. I estimated it would take another two months before I made port in Mumbai. But no sooner had the thought entered my head than I spat it out, for we sailors are as superstitious as medieval monks.

Not without reason.

In the blue-grey hours of 28 January, right before the sky started to brighten, the wind reared up. I had read the weather charts and knew what was coming. Another cold front. And it was bringing a gale.

## The Lost City of Atlantis

While bounty hunters are still raking the ocean's depths for the soggy rubble of Atlantis, most historians agree that no such island city ever existed. The Greek philosopher, Plato, was the only one who wrote about it 2300 years ago, and he must have framed it as a tale of caution against greed.

But a 'Lost City' has been discovered deep in the Atlantic basin and it is bustling with life—microscopic life! Discovered in 2000, Lost City is the name given to a hydrothermal vent field located on an underwater mountain called the Atlantis Massif.

When seawater seeps into the earth's hot mantle, the gas and energy formed by their meeting rise back up in the form of tall white spires or carbonate chimneys. The hydrogen and methane gases released through these 'chimneys' help trillions of microbes thrive, making this Lost City far more interesting to scientists than the legend of Plato, for they believe it can tell them how life on Earth itself originated.

As always, it started low and reedy like a mild note from a bamboo flute. Then, within the time it would take me to sing 'Blow the Man Down', it was a full-blown blast from the bell of a tuba. Hissing, roaring and bellowing by turn, the wind scaled up to 55 knots. Another Force 10! I knew its plans. It would roll in from the north-west, stirring up a storm for a day or more. Then, after a brief lull of about six hours, it would shift to the south-west and blow again. The waves would faithfully follow it, banking up 6 to 8 m and rising to as high as 20!

To ease off the wind, I attempted a new configuration with the sails. Seasoned sailors know instinctively how to trim them. We spend years learning the language of the wind; we know what it says when it sings or screams. And with what ears do we listen? What else, but the sails!

It's not just a matter of knowing which sails to use (there are several), but also know how to angle them and just how much of them to open out. When sailors trim their sails—reefing or unreeling the mainsail, angling the jib or gybing the spinnaker—they're only trying to listen better. Because only when they understand what the wind's saying will they know how to respond.

That morning, however, despite my best efforts, I simply couldn't catch the wind's drift. Furious, it badgered the boat, hustling and jabbing at her until *Mhadei* started to pitch and roll at the same time in the circular and nauseating motion of a corkscrew. It was all I could do to keep my internal organs from rearranging themselves.

I started to grow frantic. I had to readjust the sails quickly and correctly. My mind raced, recalling all the sail arrangements I had learnt and practised in a similar storm. Finally, I attempted something I had never tried before. I reefed the mainsail to almost one-fourth its full size and furled the staysail to half.

It worked. *Mhadei* managed to make sense of the wind and spoke back to it in signs. Soon the two slipped into an easy chat. In a couple of hours, the sea, frightened earlier by the wind's temper, stopped heaving and gasping. Its 8-metre swells flattened out, the waves pocketed their knife-edged crests and order eventually returned to our world. Now that it had, I could finally do what needed to be done. Sleep.

In my dream, I heard a metallic voice.

'Indian Sailing Vessel. Indian Sailing Vessel.'

What sort of dream was this shaping out to be? I wondered drowsily. Then I bolted up. It wasn't a dream. It was the radio transmitter talking.

After a few seconds of silence, it stirred again, 'Indian Sailing Vessel?'

I leapt from my bunk to the navigation panel and grabbed the mic of the VHF radio.

'This is Indian Sailing Vessel *Mhadei*.'

'Indian Sailing Vessel *Mhadei*, this is Royal Air Force Hercules.'

It was a British C130J, a military aircraft of the Royal Air Force (RAF). The plane was out on a routine patrol of the seas around the Falkland Islands, in whose general direction we were heading.

I bounded up to the rails and squinted at the sky. From its far end, a plane approached. As it thundered nearer, the bulky body of the Hercules grew larger, doubling in size as it halved the distance. Its sage green lines and bottle-nose were now sharply defined in the crisp air. The RAF uses this aircraft for search and rescue operations, and to transport troops, food and cargo to places in trouble.

The four propellers of the C130J drilled the air noisily, as if boring invisible tunnels for long-distance birds. It glided low over the boat, mounting what's called a low-level flypast. As it flew, I trained my camera up on the plane, even as one of its crew trained his camera down on me. (We emailed our pictures to each other later.) That's how we got our first aerial photograph of the voyage—a bird's-eye view of the beautiful boat and her, ahem, handsome sailor. Three flypasts later, and a friendly waggle of its wings in cheerio, the C130J nosed up and swung away.

That's typically how people meet at sea. When they run into each other, they wave and gesticulate, talk on the radio or holler across the gulf—all the while each keeping to their craft. And when it's time to go, the wide ocean once again engulfs them and becomes their one and only friend.

# Penguin Country

It was the first day of March in 1833 when the HMS *Beagle* sailed into Port Louis in the Falkland Islands. The 780 islands and islets that make up this archipelago are pinned to the South Atlantic waters like a moth pinned to a spreading board. Two clusters of islands sit like wings on either side of a broad channel of water called the Falkland Sound.

On the deck of the ship, sizing up the land before him stood Charles Darwin. He was 24 years old and he was unimpressed. 'Miserable' is how he summed up the Falklands in his diary, and then elaborated: 'An undulating land, with a desolate and wretched aspect, is everywhere covered by a peaty soil and wiry grass, of one monotonous brown colour.'

But the geologist nevertheless went to work. He diligently collected rock samples and fossils (some estimated to be 400 million years old!) and recorded all the animals he saw: rabbits, bulls, penguins, horses, carrion-eating caracaras and geese. A few of these he dissected right there, the rest he pickled to study back home in London.

A full year later, the *Beagle* doubled back to the islands, and once more, Darwin went about collecting and cataloguing for all he was worth. He noted the size and shape of the warrah, the Falklands wolf that's now extinct. He made close acquaintance with the flightless steamer duck, landing a mighty blow on its head with his geologist's hammer—the better to inspect its insides. He also met the Magellanic penguin, noting that the bird brayed on land—earning it the rude nickname 'jackass penguin'.

Exactly 180 years after Darwin, I found myself on those very waters. I had initially intended to sail close enough to Port Stanley—the

capital of the Falkland Islands—to catch a glimpse of it. But the winds shifted and I found myself too far from land to see either 'peaty soil' or 'wiry grass'.

And yet I saw it clearly in my mind's eye. For I had been there before. Only three years ago I'd flown into Port Stanley to assist Captain Dilip Donde, who had stopped at the islands during his circumnavigation. As Darwin had observed, it was truly a bleak, wind-swept terrain with hardly any trees. The few that did stick their necks out either slanted drunkenly to one side or were pulled clean out of the ground and swept away by the tearing gales that ceaselessly circled the place.

But what was lacking in plants was more than made up by animals. Sheep and penguins, namely. There were something like 167 sheep to every human being on the islands. So if the human population was 3000, the sheep population was half a million. The penguin population, it turned out, was double that. In fact, road signs tacked up and down the countryside warned people against trespassing—not into human, but into penguin and sheep territory!

I headed to Sea Lion Island to meet some of the animals. Scattered among the sleek southern sea lions and barrel-chested southern elephant seals were three of the Falklands' five penguin species—the southern rockhopper, the Magellanic and the gentoo. Picking my way among the thousands on the beach, kitted out in their tight glossy black coats and white-fronted dress-shirts, I felt grossly underdressed, as though I were crashing a business party. Holding my breath, I tried to be as inconspicuous as possible, for never before had I mingled with such sharp-suited company.

Lost in thoughts of the Falklands, I almost forgot where I was. In the South Atlantic Ocean of course, about to cross the 34th meridian west of Greenwich. Right on cue. My thirty-fourth birthday was about to dawn.

When it did, on 5 February, the sky made it a morning I would never forget. It wheeled out the sun like a giant butternut cake that dripped a golden glaze over the sea. Buoyed by sunny skies, I was cheered further by a blizzard of birthday emails and phone calls.

I had planned my birthday banquet well in advance, and, being a party of one, had every crumb of fresh and frozen food entirely to myself!

The birthday menu (for I have not one, but several sweet teeth) was as follows:

- Freeze-dried ice cream
- Apricot crumble
- Kheer
- Halwa
- Fresh apples

## Sailors' Superstitions

When it comes to superstitions, sailors can compile an alphabetical encyclopaedia. Beliefs differ from place to place and age to age. It starts right at the gangplank, when some sailors enter a ship on their right foot, believing the left to bring bad luck. Ancient sailors also considered it bad luck to bring the bones of the dead, or worse, a corpse, on board, for that would invite a storm. And if by chance, a storm did arrive, with or without a dead body, they'd cast lots to see who was responsible for it. Whoever drew a lot three times in a row was declared the culprit, lowered on a raft and sacrificed to the storm. Whistling would also raise a storm. And at the time of departure, saying 'goodbye' might prevent the boat from returning home. The preferred farewell is 'May you have fair winds and following seas' . . . a bit of a mouthful, but better than 'see you never'!

The apples were a gift from a friend in Goa. 'I know fresh food doesn't last long at sea, but these I guarantee will survive well into the journey,' she promised. And they did! What she did was pretty nifty: She placed three fresh apples in a can along with a lit candle and then shut and sealed the container. The lit candle ate up all the oxygen and stopped the apples from browning and going bad. Simple science!

The *Mhadei*, in the meanwhile, had a gift of her own. She covered 204 nautical miles in twenty-four hours, skimming the surface like a marble on glass. Sailing like this would get me across the Atlantic before the night was out!

# The Cross-Ocean Race for Tea

We were now three-quarters of the way home, and I could almost smell the tea steaming up from Mumbai. The city told time by tea, which reminded me of another story.

In the middle of the 1800s, the sea lanes shooting out of America and Europe all the way to China had transformed into racetracks. There were no chalked lines on the waters, but the sprinters could be seen from miles away. Three-masted tea clippers! With their three dozen puffed sails and their pointed bowsprits, these ships were the athletes of the nineteenth-century ocean.

Every year, late April, even as the first young leaves were being freshly plucked from the tea gardens of China, the tea clippers lay waiting for them at the docks of Canton and Fuzhou in the south-east. In a few days, the tea would make its way into their holds, packed tight into square wooden chests. By the end of May or early June, their bellies bursting with 50,000 kilos of paper-dry leaves, the clippers would blaze away down the South China Sea, across the Indian Ocean, around the Cape of Good Hope and up the Atlantic.

Each clipper wanted to be the first to reach America or England. For the first to arrive would receive a handsome reward—prize money for the crew! So they clipped across the ocean at a speed of 10–12 knots, often within sight of each other, yet all the while straining to edge ahead. Over forty sailors fanned out across each ship, shimmying up the masts to tend the sails or heading down into the holds to check on their precious cargo. For if seawater got in, or the boxes toppled over and spilled the tea, all would be lost.

Even on the water, they raced past milestones. And when they were spotted by lookouts on land, news of which ship was ahead of which was quickly telegrammed to London or New York, and the excitement back home doubled by the day.

Within a hundred short days, the race would be over. The swiftest ships, driven by the south-east trade winds, managed to dash across the finish line in ninety-nine, or ninety-seven or even eighty-one days! Then, the reception they received!

In London, crowds of people streamed to the docks the minute they heard the winning clipper was swanning up the Thames on the leash of a tugboat. Roars and cheers erupted and betting money was cheerfully pocketed, because this was, after all, a race . . . the biggest of the year . . . and wagers were made all round, just like at the races today.

However, the excitement was short-lived, and all because of a shortcut. In 1869, the Suez Canal opened in Egypt, considerably shrinking travel time between Europe and Asia. Steamships now stepped in and elbowed the great clippers out of the game. Unlike the clippers, the coal-fed steamers, cutting through the canal, could bring the tea home to London in under two months!

But while everyone could now take more tea, no one was interested in watching steamers race each other, for the fun was in watching the wind swing a ship's fortunes! And so, in a little over twenty years, the great tea races of the nineteenth century came to a tragically tepid end.

While the tea clippers were soon reduced to woodchips, one relic still stands—the black-hulled *Cutty Sark*! Docked at the Royal Museums Greenwich, people can actually enter this ship and have a look around. They can also see, but not tour it, in my living room in Kochi!

This is how I came to own the *Cutty Sark*.

Before Sagar Parikrama I, one of our practice runs with *Mhadei* took Captain Donde and me to Mauritius. There, at Port Louis (the capital), was a shop full of ships. Some were stuffed into narrow-necked glass bottles, others were mounted grandly on long wooden stands. My eyes roved this shipyard of nautical models and came to rest on a four-foot vessel with a hull made of teak, and miniature sails of canvas sitting stiffly on delicate rigging. 'That's the ship for me,' I decided then and there. I coughed up the money, had it carefully packed and stowed on our boat, and took the *Cutty Sark* all the way back to Kochi to be mounted on a mantle.

If not a car, I could at least say (with full honesty) that I owned a sailboat.

As I thought about the tea clippers racing back up the Atlantic over a century ago, I remembered the race *Mhadei* herself had run on these same waters in 2011. It was the electric Cape to Rio yacht race, a 3600-nautical mile course from Cape Town in South Africa to Rio de Janeiro on the eastern edge of Brazil.

We had set off on 11 January, with a crew of four sailors and Captain Donde at the helm. It had been decided that a race across the Atlantic would be the best way to prepare me for my upcoming circumnavigation. *Mhadei*, however, had been built for a multi-ocean marathon, not a short sea sprint. She was made for stability and endurance, not speed. Yacht races are run by boats with a more aero- and hydrodynamic design to help them cut smoothly and swiftly through the water. Racing boats are also far lighter—one the size of *Mhadei* wouldn't be half as heavy as her. So while it did disappoint us, it did not entirely crush us when a month later, on 9 February, we finished the Cape to Rio race in fifteenth place!

Barely two weeks after putting into port at Rio, I had to put out again. But this time, *I* would be the one to skipper the yacht, sailing with a full

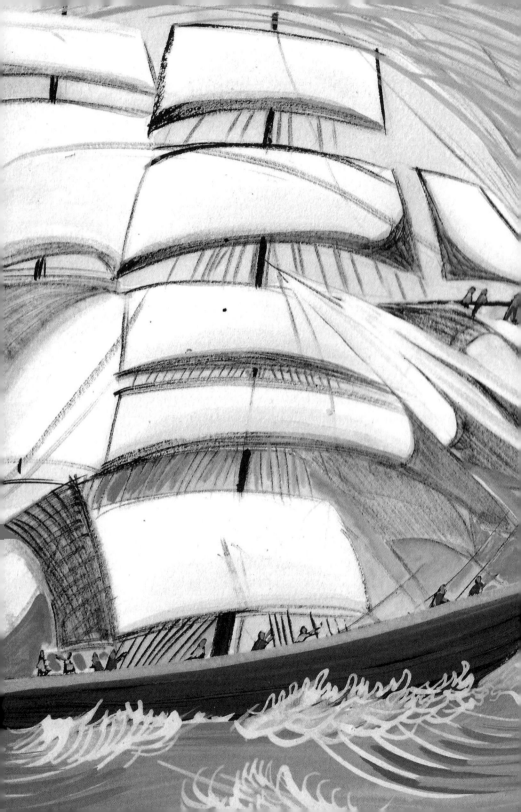

crew of one—naval officer Lieutenant Commander Gautam Khajuria. It was to be my very first command of *Mhadei* and I was nine-tenths excited and one-tenths anxious. But almost as soon as we reversed our steps from Brazil to Cape Town, the scales shifted and it was worry that kept its dead weight in my pocket the rest of the way.

For the sailing was as smooth as a whirl in a blender. No sooner had we set off than beastly headwinds rammed into us from ahead, grabbing the boat and shaking it down to the rudder. They clawed at the mainsail over and over again, and by the time we reached the middle of the Atlantic, there were two broad gashes across its face. If *that* wasn't enough, roughed up by choppy seas, *Mhadei* sprung a leak in the propeller shaft, the long cylinder that connects the engine to the fan-shaped propeller at the stern. Now any leak is bad news and if we didn't attend to it immediately, we could be in deep waters.

Lieutenant Commander Khajuria and I got to work, spending hour upon sweating hour fixing the boat's mounting problems. Seven of those hours were spent on the mast itself, climbing and descending it to replace the torn mainsail. From the mast, we moved to the engine room, where the bilge had started to flood because of the leaking shaft. I realized we could do nothing to fix it, except pump out the bilge water. This had to be done once every three hours, every single day for the length of the four weeks we sailed. And although the heavy lifting was done by an electric pump, the job still needed a human eye and hand to oversee it, which was a huge bother.

Yet, despite our troubles, we called ourselves lucky on finally mooring at Table Bay in Cape Town on 24 March. Some of the other yachts returning from the race had had a far worse time of it. The spars on the mast of one boat broke, another lost its mast entirely, one was parted from its rudder and a fourth sank altogether!

~~

On 12 February 2013, *Mhadei* crossed the 4th meridian west of Greenwich. It had been four years since she was formally inducted into the Indian Navy. Incidentally, 12 February also happens to be the birthday of Charles Darwin, whom I suspect *Mhadei* admires very much, having made a sailing pilgrimage to nearly all the places the naturalist had visited on the *Beagle*. The string of coincidences kept unravelling. *That* was also the day I was formally made skipper of the boat.

It happened soon after the Cape to Rio race. Before I headed back to Cape Town and on to Goa, Captain Donde and I decided to see the sights of Rio. On the morning of 12 February, we made our way to Sugarloaf Mountain, a tall peak that gets its name from conical blocks of sugar sold long ago. Standing on the observation deck overlooking Guanabara Bay, which was dotted with boats, we chatted about this and that as we cast our eye over the stunning view ahead of us. The Atlantic lay on one side and the soaring statue of Christ the Redeemer lay on the other.

After a pause, Captain Donde turned to me and with a half-smile said the sum total of two words: 'All yours'. Although it came as no surprise, a thrill still shot up my spine like a firecracker. I knew what the words meant. He was officially passing the boat—and baton—over to me. From then on, until the end of Sagar Parikrama II, *Mhadei* would be mine and mine alone.

# Staying Upright Is Downright Difficult

A wall, tall and black as basalt, covered the horizon from floor to ceiling—sea to sky. On the deck of his vessel, the sailor watched it and, despite the chill, broke out into a sweat. He could see it gaining on him and knew it was only a matter of time before the crash.

At last it came, the wall of storm.

The water was on the boil. Mountain waves hovered over the boat, then with bruising precision crashed down upon it, turning the brown floorboards white with spray.

The storm threw itself with a vengeance against the vessel, leaning harder and harder into it until it flattened it against the waves. The sailor's eyes shut tight. If this was the end, he did not want to see it.

By the time the waters had settled, the storm had long gone and the sailor, when he opened his eyes, was deep inside the sea.

The irony is, it was this very sailor who had named the spot that took his life. *Cabo das Tormentas.* Cape of Storms. The sailor was Bartolomeu Dias.

It was January 1488 when Dias discovered it.

It was May 1500 when he died at the Cape.

Dias was the first European to round the Cape of Good Hope, and the first to turn the southern corner of the African continent. And because

*he* had, Europeans could now bypass the difficult overland route to the East and trade (and take over) places in Arabia and Asia with little to no trouble.

Despite his great achievement, Dias's star paled in the glow of Portuguese navigators like Vasco da Gama, who, incidentally, managed to reach India only because it was Dias himself who helped pave the way into the Indian Ocean.

To add insult to injury, even the cape Dias had named was renamed. The Portuguese king, João II, Dias's patron, did not care much for the title the sailor had given the pivotal cape, the pessimistic and ill-omened *Cabo das Tormentas*. So he changed it to *Cabo da Boa Esperança*— Cape of Good Hope—hoping that good fortune would follow on the heels of the new name.

On 18 February, I thought of Bartolomeu Dias and his luckless voyage. In a day's time, *I* was about to cross those same seas.

By the noon of 19 February, I touched the longitude of the Cape.

It would be more accurate to say I *flew* into it, for a 40-knot wind rushed at me from the south-west. I swung to the south, keeping an arm's length of at least 200 nautical miles from Good Hope. If I hadn't, I might have been caught in the teeth of rough winds and steep waves that can rise as high as 100 ft nearer the cape. This lovely little sea of tranquillity is whipped up by two opposing forces of nature—a warm westward-flowing current called Agulhas and strong eastward-blowing winds. The clash of these titans is what raises hell on the waves. It is to avoid being caught in the middle of a battle between wind and current that sailors rounding the cape from west to east, sail south.

(The warm Agulhas current slides down from Mozambique and Madagascar, all the way to the Cape, and shoots out east again, tracing an acute angle on the water.)

This region of the ocean is a hothouse of storms, with almost two rising up every week!

While I'd moved out of the way of the current, I hadn't moved out of the way of the wind. Here too it spun, climbing steadily to 45 knots . . . then 48 . . . then 50. In the meanwhile, the swell underfoot stood at 30–33 ft, as high as telephone poles! I reefed the mainsail to the maximum to put as little fabric in the way of the wind as possible. I did this by lowering the sail to its fourth reefing line on the boom. Reefing a mainsail is like lowering window blinds. Except, you don't pull a string to send the blind up, you drop the halyard to bring the sail down. Four reefs on the mainsail fold it up to nearly a quarter of its full size.

When the wind has both hands on the hull and is pushing the boat as fast as it can go, a full mainsail will not make it go any faster. It can, in fact, have the opposite effect. It can stress the rudder and the rigging, and bring the boat to heel dangerously or bend over to one side. Sometimes, the boat can turn all the way around and point right to the wind!

But reefing the mainsail wasn't enough. I had to shorten the staysail too, which was behind the mainsail near the bow. All that time, *Mhadei* bounced on the water like a seal on a trampoline. Although I did manage to stay on the flat of my feet, it was only by bending and bracing my body like a breakdancer that I kept upright.

## Adamastor

According to the sixteenth-century Portuguese poem *Os Luciadas*, the Cape of Good Hope is not just any old landform, but a wild titan called Adamastor set permanently in stone. He sits hard and heavy-browed, his rugged body forming the headland of the great cape, closely guarding the trapdoor between the Atlantic and Indian Ocean. When a sailor dares to cross over, Adamastor plucks himself up in a temper, gathering clouds and stirring storms, hell-bent on sending the sailor to a watery death.

Finally, after about four windy and rackety hours, we scudded past the cape without losing body or boat to the water. Dias's fate was not to be mine.

*Mhadei* now arrowed in the direction of that true southernmost cape of Africa—Agulhas. I had hoped to leave the torments of Good Hope behind me, but little did I know that the Cape of Needles, as Agulhas is called, had a worse sting in store.

Crossing the 20th meridian east in the early hours of the evening of 19 February, I had now formally and finally stepped out of the Atlantic and into the Indian Ocean.

That, unfortunately, changed nothing.

The ocean's brow was still furrowed; its white crests knitted together in long frown lines. But it was only a scowl, not real fury. The winds were large but not rough and the sky appeared even-tempered. Taupe stratus clouds stretched flat like dough, heavy but unthreatening.

Or so it seemed.

While I wasn't looking, the big baker in the sky quietly gathered up the clouds into a colossal heap. Then with one mighty motion punched down, knocking the wind right out of it. It hurtled in at 70 knots, falling upon us with the force of a wrecking ball. *Mhadei* tipped over without warning, making a 50° angle with the water. I tipped over too, but before I could fall overboard, I grabbed hold of a winch, one of the cylindrical fixtures around the boat to which the ropes are fastened.

I hadn't expected this sudden change of sky, so I hadn't strapped on my rough weather harness that would have secured me to the boat. These harnesses, or jacket leashes, are clipped by rope to any part of the boat so that if it suddenly rolls or yaws and the sailor pitches over, he or she is held fast by the harness and can climb back aboard.

After what seemed like a few short hours, but must have only been several long seconds, *Mhadei* righted herself with effort. I righted myself too and wobbled down into the safety of the cabin.

Outside, the waves tossed themselves on board, grabbing hold of the deck with slick fingers. One of them reached right up to the furled genoa at the bow, and managed to prise open a small bit of its midsection. Within seconds, the wind discovered the opening and dove in, filling the gaps between the folds with its bulk. More wind flooded it, inflating the sail's ends like an hourglass. Still held fast around the middle by rope, the genoa, which was tethered to the mast, pulled and strained at the pole. Inside the cabin, I could feel the mast juddering, and instantly knew something was wrong.

With speed, I ducked out and, dodging the bearish wind, unfastened the ropes that bound the genoa. Like the great wing of a wandering albatross, the sail shook free and bloomed. The wind, now caught in its belly, strained hard against it, causing the mast and boat to rattle violently. Another skipper, on another journey, described this motion perfectly when he compared it to the hand of a powerful god holding the boat by the tip of the mast and giving it a vigorous shakedown.

For the first time in over a hundred days, I started to pray. 'Don't let this be the end,' I begged the Hand. 'Let go and let me get on with it!'

But the wind did not pull back. It sharpened itself into a blade edge and with a vengeance slashed at the Dacron, the fabric of the sail. It nicked slowly at first, making long narrow slits, but these widened until after a while, all 800 sq. ft of the sail were turned into a triangular frame of streamers. The carnage had lasted no more than thirty minutes!

Now, finally, like a bull at the close of a bloody fight, the wind snorted and sank down, leaving the sea and me breathless with relief.

# Mapping the Ocean

## Fifth and Final Leg: Cape of Good Hope to Mumbai
## 20 February 2013 to 31 March 2013

'Welcome back to your home waters. All three great capes passed correctly. Well done.'

The email from Sir Robin Knox-Johnston had been one of the first to arrive on 19 February, the same day the wind had made seaweed of the genoa. Although we made it safely past Good Hope and Agulhas, my nerves were still thrumming. It would take long hours, perhaps long days, for them to settle down. I was so shaken, the ocean and sky appeared fragmented, like the trillion pieces of a jigsaw puzzle that had been flung up and hadn't yet fallen back into place.

On the back of Sir RXJ's email came a barrage of other messages, congratulating me on crossing the final Great Cape and whistling their welcome to the Indian Ocean. The world slowly started to piece itself together again.

Yet, of all the messages I received, it was Sir Robin's that thrilled me most. After all, wasn't he the first of us!

~~~

On 14 June 1968, nine sailors cast off from Falmouth Harbour in England to take part in the world's first non-stop solo circumnavigation, the Sunday Times Golden Globe Race. Only one finished it.

After 312 days at sea, to the roaring applause of Britain and the world, Sir Robin sailed back home in his Bermudan ketch, a two-masted sailboat called *Suhaili*.

The sailors of the Golden Globe Race had no satellite technology to guide them (marine GPS only became available in 1990). And they had no gadgets to warn them of coming storms. To make matters worse, Robin's ketch was bedevilled by multiple problems during the race—from the radio breaking down to the self-steering mechanism going kaput. Despite all this, the 29-year-old sailor soldiered on, and ended up bagging the very first Golden Globe trophy, and its cash prize of 5000 pounds! Incidentally, Sir Robin's 32-foot yacht— built from a single, six-ton log of teak—was born in a shipyard in Mumbai!

Years after sailing out of India in his newly built yacht, Sir Robin would return to the country to test the springs of another boat—the *Mhadei*. In 2009, before Captain Donde embarked on Sagar Parikrama, the navy requested Sir Robin to give the boat his thumbs up. So the veteran sailor, along with Captain Donde, took *Mhadei* out to sea for a short spin, and when they returned Sir Robin declared her to be shipshape and good to go.

As far as heroes went, Sir Robin stood right there next to Admiral Awati. *Perhaps one day I'll sail the Golden Globe Race too*, I often thought. As far as goals went, it was pretty ambitious, but one has to dream big.

On the morning of 20 February, another email dropped into my inbox from Sir Robin.

'I have just updated the list of people who have circumnavigated solo south of the three great capes . . . This brings the list to 199 . . . Unless someone else creeps in from another source, of which I currently have no knowledge, the position of 200th on the list is the next one and waiting for you.

Go for it!'

RKJ

This last leg of the voyage was going to be the trickiest of all, for the Indian Ocean is no swimming pool. It's a minefield of fronts, cyclones, currents, counter-currents, squalls, trade winds, shipping lanes, fishing boats, doldrums, tropical heat, islands and banks, and not least of the lot—pirates. A 5000-mile obstacle-course-of-an-ocean! As I gazed ahead, its grey-blue waves appeared like sinuous snakes in the great Indian game of snakes and ladders. One miscalculated move would take me straight down a serpent's belly, swallowing days of progress and slowing my run to the finish line.

But then, I'd sailed two-thirds of the world without a chopping board . . . what were pirates in comparison!

It was smooth sailing for the next couple of days. There was still a great deal of work to be done, though. I had my logbook to fill. This journal—the boat's private diary—recorded a daily catalogue of weather conditions, coordinates, sightings (of ship, sea life, land or lighthouse), depth records, change of course, change of sails, running hours of engine and generator, emails, phone calls, and all accidents and incidents on board—from a torn genoa to a broken pump. In sum, a complete catalogue of every day at sea.

Sailors through the centuries have faithfully recorded every high and low, every romantic and revolting detail of their journey in their logs. For example, on 19 August 1856, the logs of the *Chasca* forlornly stated: '*Our ship is overrun with all kinds of Insects, Ants, Flys, Musqueto, Cockroach, Rats, etc. You cannot put eny thing in to your*

*Mouth without getting a lot of Ants & as for Musquetos they will not let you have eny peace.'*

Before written records, however, the sailor's log took the form of spoken stories, and these accounts were shared with their clan to guide them in their own explorations for food and later, for land. Instructions on how far one should sail from home to spear a shark changed over time to how far one should sail to discover a new country.

At no other time in the long history of navigation did this information become as valuable as during the Age of Sail, from the sixteenth to the nineteenth century. During this era, the explorer's practice of observing, recording, charting, naming and recounting the sea and its parts was honed to a fine science, only to gain the lead in the Great Global Race for new trade routes and colonies.

## The Cantino Planisphere

Spies in the Age of Sail were routinely deployed to copy, buy or steal important sea charts. One of these was the famed Cantino Planisphere. (A planisphere is a sphere represented as a plane or flat surface).

This Portuguese chart, drawn up in 1502, consisted of six pieces of parchment attached to a large, 4 × 8 foot canvas sheet. It was important because it offered a mine of information not only about the newly discovered New World, the Americas, but also about new Portuguese sea routes, like Vasco da Gama's to India in 1497. What's more, it was the first map to picture the Tropics, the Arctic Circle and the equator.

Some say the planisphere was stolen from the Portuguese by a man called Alberto Cantino, others say Cantino had a map-maker steal into a map room and copy the drawings. Whichever version is true, Cantino only acted on the instructions of the Duke of Ferrara in Italy.

The chart was lost in the labyrinths of time until it was rediscovered in the nineteenth century—on the wall of a butcher's shop! It thankfully hangs today in the Biblioteca Estense, a library and museum in Modena, Italy.

As each new wave of navigators added to this ocean of knowledge, the charts and maps they drew—of sea lanes, latitudes, reefs, rivers and harbours—were guarded with slit-eyed jealousy by their country's kings. These were, after all, treasure maps pointing the way to fabled riches in new lands. Why, then, would any monarch allow such hard-won knowledge to come into the hands of a rival? It was, in fact, not uncommon for one crafty kingdom to fox another by delivering muddled maps into their laps, only to strand their sailors at sea.

To this long documentary of the ocean, I added my own blogs, videos and photographs. By now, my social media accounts had over 15 million views, and my followers had swelled to 70,000. It felt as though a crowd was following *Mhadei* and me. Every dolphin I spotted, or storm I saw, they saw too. It was flattering at first to have such a large audience. It felt as though I was standing at the stern of my little boat, shouting about my life through a megaphone to all those people following us. But over time, I lost sight of the crowds and it was just the sea, *Mhadei* and me. I still kept telling my story though—not because it needed to be heard, but because it had to be told.

As I drew nearer home, that strange feeling reappeared. Relief and dread, like siblings who fought but couldn't be separated, took up room in my heart. Excitement at approaching the finish line was oddly entangled with regret at having to leave the road I had grown to love. That I would, in a few weeks, turn sharply left, off the thoroughfare of the ocean and into the side street of the sea, brought an unexpected sadness upon me.

I didn't look forward to the crowds, the clamour and the endless conversations that waited for me on land. I had spoken little over the last three months . . . stray words to ground control, to strangers on the radar and fictional friends on the journey. But I had only really found common tongue with the ocean. And I was afraid that once back on land, I was going to lose it.

# Circling Back

A great calamity was about to strike two cities by the Salt Sea, what we know today as the Dead Sea. None but one man called Lot knew what was coming—blazing fireballs from the sky! 'The cities will burn like bonfires,' angels warned him. 'But don't worry, you and your family can escape, without so much as a blister.' They tacked another warning to the first: 'When you go down the road, DO NOT, we repeat, DO NOT look back at the cities. For if you do . . . well, don't say we didn't warn you!'

That night, Lot and his family bundled a few clothes, some bread and cheese and ran for their lives. As they bolted down the road, they heard the sizzling and crackling and sputtering of sparks. 'Whatever you do, don't look back,' the man reminded his wife and daughters as they sped away from the blaze.

His wife, unfortunately, was a curious creature. She had never seen a city burn before and thought she'd steal a quick glance. But no sooner did she swivel her head, she felt a tingling in her toes. It climbed up her waist, then her arms and her neck, and before her mouth could cry out, *it* too was caught fast by the curse.

She had turned into a rock-hard pillar of salt.

Were *Mhadei* and I turning to salt too? For what was it if not salt encrusting the metal rail of the gunwale? And salt on the masts, the hull, the sails and even in my hair and my beard—salt everywhere, covering everything in a white, sticky, sodium stubble.

As we progressed towards the equator, the days grew steadily warmer, with temperatures climbing to the high 30s. Gone was the cold, but gone

too were the rains of the South Atlantic that had washed down the boat and dissolved the salt that lingered after every lick of the sea. For every time the sea sprayed us—which was every minute of the journey—it left crumbs of salt behind, making everything, including my skin moist and sticky to the touch. It's why the old Bible story of Lot and his wife came back to mind.

Only four months ago, I was preparing for cold, drizzly days. Now I was doing the reverse. I started to pack the boots and oilskin jackets away, for the days ahead would bring nothing but heat and sweat.

I was down to a pair of cotton shorts and vest—the bare necessities to keep the dignity of the Indian Navy unsullied. We were returning to the busy intersections of the ocean and one never knew when a passing vessel would decide to stop and size me up.

Fifteen balmy nights had passed since the Cape of Good Hope. It could have been fifteen fortnights, for time stretched like honey, long and gluey.

One such night, I took my dinner up to the prow just as the sun had started to dissolve at the far end of the ocean. Its colour seeped into the water as if from a teabag, in deep ginger rivulets. I had cooked a handful of rice, peeled open a can of tuna, and spooned a large dollop of bora pickle into my bowl. The pickle was a home-made gift from a friend's cook in Goa. I've always believed that if you want to brighten up a boring meal, serve it with pickle, any pickle.

The sky was now an iron sieve, sifting starlight into long silver strands on the ocean. And the wind, tetchy only weeks ago, now lightly fanned my face. As I ate my meal, listening to the quiet splash of the waves, I knew I wouldn't trade this moment for all the diamonds in Botswana.

~~~

After a long and satisfying dinner, I decided to get back to work. There was unfinished business on the boat and it made itself known with an urgent, peevish flapping. I looked up in irritation. The shreds of the mangled genoa, torn at Agulhas, made rude gestures in the breeze. 'That blasted thing!' I muttered.

Since the wind had ripped it on the day of our cape crossing, I'd made no fewer than eleven attempts to cut off what remained of the tattered sail. Its strips had curled around the forestay, the steel rod that runs from the near top of the mast, all the way down to the bow. The forestay was part of the standing rigging of the boat—the fixed ropes, wires and rods that support the mast and sails.

Scaling the mast was never easy, even in a bosun's chair. I knew this already from my first trek up, but I had hoped the climb would get easier with practice. Eleven climbs later, I was still wrong.

I had made it a point to go up the mast on low-wind days so that the boat wouldn't rock and make the task more dangerous. I also chose to climb at sunset to escape the day's heat. Yet, no matter how well calibrated the conditions, every single mount was exhausting and demanded a horrible half hour. Once level with the strips of sail, I'd carefully snip away at the fabric with a pair of scissors.

Tonight, I hoped, would be the final trim.

I heaved myself up, for what I prayed would be the last mast climb of the expedition. My legs by now were two quivering straws, bent out of shape from the long, body-bashing journey so far. Yet, they managed to hold fast to the mast while my hands worked away with the scissors. It was slow snipping in the light of my head torch, but I kept working until I finally made it to the genoa's last stubborn strands and set them free.

The first time I'd scaled the mast I received such a battering, I thought I'd never make it to the top. But then I did, and the view was so heart-stopping, I forgot all the tortures of the climb and went into poetic

raptures. This time, I did not stop to gaze at the sea, or write poems, or paint pictures, or sing songs or do any of those things people do when they're gobsmacked. Because I wasn't. My body had started to buckle from exhaustion, and all I wanted to do was shimmy back down safely and slip into my narrow bunk. And that is exactly what I did.

~~~

After I entered the Indian Ocean, I had several possible routes laid out before me, but only one obvious course: to sail in a near-straight line to the 54th longitude, keeping well below the 35th latitude. From there, I would angle sharply north towards the Indian subcontinent.

Anyone tracking this route on a map would be surprised to find I hadn't taken the quicker path up the Mozambique Channel, between the south-east coast of Africa and Madagascar. There were several reasons I gave that sea lane a wide berth. For one, the southward-bound Agulhas Current would make the sail up a hairy challenge. The other difficulty was the strong headwinds spinning off the Mascarene High, near the Mascarene archipelago. Located between the latitudes 20–40° south and longitudes 45–100° east, the Mascarene High is a high-pressure zone in the South Indian Ocean that nudges the summer monsoon winds towards India.

Apart from the Agulhas Current and the headwinds, other pebbles in my path were container ships and fishing vessels that crowded these waters like toy boats in a park pond. The Mozambique Channel is, after all, one of the oldest and busiest sea lanes in the world—even Vasco da Gama passed through it when sailing to India. Pirates lurked there too, making the islands that dotted the channel, like the Comoros, their hideout and hostage point.

Not least of my concerns was the size of the channel itself. Should the weather take a turn for the worse, I would be stuck between rocks and several hard places—namely the coast, and the hard hulls of 10,000-ton container ships. The 1600 km-long channel becomes a bottleneck at its narrowest point, which is only about 400 km wide. This would make manoeuvring in bad weather as tricky as trying to do backflips in a bathtub.

The route I eventually chose led me to the lip of the south-east trade winds. These constant currents of air put their weight behind the boat and pushed *Mhadei* towards the equatorial doldrums. Although we were now sprinting on the water, we could have galloped, had we had the genoa. But we made good distance nonetheless, covering 150 nautical miles a day. On 3 March, we reached the 54th meridian and turned sharply left, up towards the Indian subcontinent.

A week later, for the second time on the expedition, we crossed the Tropic of Capricorn, and if I squinted really hard, I could almost see the broad back of the Gateway of India in the far distance.

## Mascarene Islands

The Mascarene Islands, in the Western Indian Ocean, get their name from the sixteenth-century Portuguese explorer, Pedro Mascarenhas. These islands—Mauritius, Reunion and Rodrigues—lie along a submarine ridge called the Seychelles-Mauritius Plateau. One of the famous (former) inhabitants of Mauritius is the dodo—famous because it is extinct, along with its cousin, the Rodrigues solitaire of Rodrigues Island. Both were hunted out of existence by colonizers!

# Close Shave with a Ship

If you take a step back and look at the map of the Indian Ocean, you'll notice it forms the letter 'M'. Two shoulders peak on either side of the V-neck of India, one making the left arm of Arabia and Eastern Africa, the other the right arm of Myanmar, Thailand and Malaysia. And in this alphabet soup of an ocean are sprinkled thousands of islands.

For centuries, these islands were stepping stones for traders and colonizers who played a cut-throat game of hopscotch as they jumped from island to island on their way to the Asian and African continents. The islands started as wooded waypoints, stocking food and water for passing ships. But over time, they were permanently settled and became towns and eventually nations, like the Maldives, Mauritius and Madagascar—the island-nations I was about to encounter.

Just like no two seas are alike, no two islands are the same. Some, like the Maldives, are formed of coral. Others, like Mauritius, are the cooled rock of volcanic eruptions. Still others, like Madagascar, are the granite breakaway of continents. Even though the rounded ocean hides it from view, my GPS told me this last island, Madagascar, was within Olympic-swimming distance should I have wanted to reach it by breaststroke.

As a young cadet, Madagascar was the first foreign country I had visited. It was the most spectacular place I had ever seen. Bloated baobabs held up the sky and bandit-faced lemurs stared me down as I poked around the island, my pockets jingling with Malagasy francs (now Malagasy ariary). I'd read that 90 per cent of Madagascar's animals, fungi and plants were found nowhere else on the planet, making this the world's fourth largest island, also one of its most unique.

To think its earliest settlers were a group of plucky Austronesians who sailed all the way around from Borneo, on the other side of the Indian Ocean. Talk about long-distance travel! When I first visited Madagascar, I saw it with the goggle eyes of a tourist. Only much later did I learn of the troubles brewing there—the illegal trafficking of endangered lemurs and ochre-backed ploughshare tortoises; the logging of its purple-hearted rosewood trees; and the clearing of its tropical jungles for the cultivation of rice. *Would I recognize Madagascar if I visited it twenty years from now?* I wondered ruefully. I was afraid I would not.

I sailed past Madagascar and into the Mascarene archipelago. On 11 March, as I steered through the imaginary gateway formed by the islands of Mauritius on the west and Rodrigues on the east, a Dornier aircraft from the National Coast Guard of Mauritius flew past. A bird from my own flock! It seemed as if whole centuries had passed since I'd strapped myself into the cockpit of a Dornier. To now see its familiar grey bottle-nose sniffing me out deep at sea made me grin. The welcome parade had begun.

~~~

On the afternoon of 13 March, a merchant ship stacked high with enormous blue and red steel containers like giant Lego blocks, sailed into view. Her hull was painted the colour of a muddy sky and the letters M O L hung long and white on her port and starboard sides. She was the MOL *Distinction*. We each identified our vessels and coordinates as maritime rules require us to do. And then the conversation on the wireless started to sound a bit like a knock-knock joke.

MOL *Distinction*: 'Request next port of call.'

*Mhadei*: 'Mumbai.'

MOL *Distinction*: 'Request port of departure.'

*Mhadei*: 'Mumbai.'

MOL *Distinction*: 'No, sir. That's your destination. Request port of departure.'

*Mhadei*: 'I repeat, port of departure was Mumbai.'

MOL *Distinction*: 'Then what is your next port of call?'

*Mhadei*: 'Next port of call is also Mumbai.'

The officer thought I was being cheeky until I patiently laid it all out for him with every detail of the expedition, but the diagram.

I first saw the ship belowdecks, on *Mhadei*'s AIS. A black speck crawling across the radar's web like a harmless house spider. Only she wasn't. She was a hulking 42,100-ton vessel, crossing rapidly from my port side to starboard side, not less than 500 m away.

I had my closest point of approach (CPA) alert set to a 5-mile radius. This meant any vessel approaching *Mhadei* within that close circle would warn me well in advance, and we would move out of each other's way. I had spotted the MOL *Distinction* as soon as she entered the circle, and radioing the ship, alerted the officer on watch to my position.

'Can you see me on your AIS?' I asked the officer.

Sometimes a small vessel does not show up on a larger vessel's AIS, particularly if their tracking technology is old and outdated.

'Yes, we will keep clear, don't worry,' came the reply.

'Do you need me to change course?' I asked again. One of us would have to alter our course to avoid a close shave.

'We will keep clear,' the officer promised.

But the ship did not alter course. She inched nearer and nearer, and just as I prepared to steer clear of her, it was she who throttled up at the last moment to give me right of way. Even though I was in no danger of colliding with the container ship—being perfectly capable of steering safely away—a time-honoured rule of the ocean demanded that the ship step aside for me!

Just like on land, seafarers also follow 'rules of the road'. These rules decide which vessel should change its course, speed up or slow down to avoid a collision. One of these rules insists that a sailboat should be given right of way by a motored vessel. Or in this case, an 866-ft diesel-powered leviathan must step aside for a 56-ft wind-powered Lilliputian.

Despite the immenseness of the ocean and the maze of technology built into modern ships to help them navigate safely—GPS, radio communication and AIS systems—collisions do still happen, sending both containers and lives tumbling overboard. And when this happens, fingers generally point in one direction—to a single pair of bleary eyes! If the officer in charge of keeping vigil over the tracking screens has fallen asleep, or steps out for a loo break or simply doesn't notice the approaching blip on the radar, a ship may continue to sail cheerfully right into the path of a passing vessel.

## Container Ships

Merchant ships are the lumbering container trucks of the ocean's expressways, ferrying millions of enormous metal boxes across the world every year. The goods they carried were worth over 14 trillion US dollars in 2019. Container ships are the cheapest way to transport things over long distances. Where once, carracks and clippers raced the seas bearing salt and cedar, today container ships take their place, carrying everything people are willing to buy, from monoculture bananas to mass-produced bandanas.

Sometimes, however, a ship's technology simply cannot pick up every single vessel in its vicinity. At other times, weather conditions are to blame—storms with vaulting waves, pitching seas and blinding rain that reduce visibility to near zero, throw the most obedient of ships off course and into the path of fellow travellers. Then again, the sacrificial goat may be a simple fishing boat that lacks the sophisticated gadgetry of a larger vessel. It isn't uncommon for these little boats to be crushed by powerful merchant ships, or even blindly tossed aside by the waters of their wake.

Thankfully, I was both seen and heard by the watchful officer on MOL *Distinction*. As she slugged out of sight, a thought dropped suddenly like a little coconut on my head: that was the first vessel I had hooked eyes on since *Erica XII* at Cape Horn, half a world away! Civilization was just around the corner and it started to make me very nervous.

# Not a Drop to Drink

We were flying towards the equator on the wings of the trade winds beating in from the south-east. By flying, I mean we were sailing swiftly . . . but by no means smoothly. A wind and swell hit the boat right in the beam, the widest part of the hull above the waterline, making it roll from side to side like a drunken barrel. It made me so nauseous, my head felt like a pot of steaming cabbage soup! Fighting the urge to tip over the side of the boat and feed myself to the fish, I pinned myself to the navigation table instead and pored over the electronic weather charts. The boat, in the meanwhile, rolled and rolled.

The challenge now was to not only pick a route through the changing wind and the advancing South Equatorial Current, but to manoeuvre between islands, islets, underwater shoals, banks and reefs that were laid out neatly like a devil's snare just beneath the surface. I had to carefully pick my way through these shallow waters or risk running the boat aground, for the memory of my sticky sail two years ago from Cape Town to Goa still clung like a barnacle to my mind.

This is what had happened . . . We were sailing in waters almost 6500 ft deep, when all of a sudden, the echo sounder signalled immediate danger. (The echo sounder is the instrument that measures the depth of the water, from the bottom of the boat to the seabed.) The sound waves that echoed back up had rapidly shrunk! We had strayed over a sea bank, the shallow part of a seabed, which now sat no lower than 16 ft below the hull! Any closer and the bank could graze the bottom of the boat, perhaps ripping through its hull or even cracking the mast with the force of impact. It was with my heart beating wildly in my mouth and my intestines knotting even further that I shakily steered *Mhadei* back into deeper and safer waters.

This time, I knew better. Memorizing the routing charts and pilot handbooks, I plotted what I knew to be a reliable route through the Nazareth and Saya de Malha banks of the Mascarene Plateau.

The Saya de Malha bank, incidentally, is one of the largest shallow tropical marine ecosystems in the world, a vast 40,808 sq. km area of submerged life. And most of it is green! That's because a large part of this bank is covered in seagrass, making it the largest seagrass meadow on Earth!

I was, by now, almost out of the grasp of the south-east trade winds and about to be gripped by the north-westerlies.

Up until then, the trades had been strong enough to whisk me along without the need for the large genoa. But I was now entering a zone of light winds, and would need all the help I could get from the sails to catch what I could of the breeze. On one calm day when the wind said little, I went belowdecks to fetch up one of the spare genoas, a carbon Spectra sail. Spectra is one of the lightest and strongest fibres in the world, ten times stronger than steel.

It was a three-year-old sail, but I chose it from among the newer models because of its light weight, which made it easy to hoist. What's more, the sail had served me well on another, older voyage and I had come to trust it.

With some effort, I lugged the 30 kg fabric up to the deck and began the elaborate drill of rigging the lines. The Spectra, however, had no intention of being put to work. And I soon saw why when I started to hoist it.

A scattering of fine, rootlike lines fanned out across the cloth, letting in little pockets of breeze, even as the sail attempted to stand up stoutly to the wind. I nearly beat my head against the mast! We had failed to examine this sail for wear and tear before the voyage, and as anyone could tell by looking at it—it was worn and torn. The tired fibre had frayed in places or been nibbled away by mould, and little gashes across its surface made it downright useless.

I glumly took the Spectra down, stowed it back in its sail-bag and rigged a newer, slightly heavier Dacron in its place. The sun had set by this time, and after the exertions of the evening, I needed a pick-me-up. Like popcorn.

There's no snack I love more in the world and I made sure to carry at least 200 sachets of it on the voyage. And so it was that evening that I devoured a packet even as the genoa above me swallowed the wind.

~~~

*Water, water everywhere,*

*And all the boards did shrink.*

*Water, water everywhere,*

*Nor any drop to drink.*

('The Rime of the Ancient Mariner', 1834)

No lines of sea poetry have been preserved so well as these by Samuel Taylor Coleridge. This idle thought did not occur to me on 17 March. For when disaster strikes, it isn't accompanied by a poem, no matter how fitting.

And on 17 March, disaster struck.

As we neared the equator, the heat had started to brick up like a dense wall, and I found myself reaching for a gulp of water every other hour. I was worried because my stock of water bottles was steadily dwindling. While l could bank on the water in the storage tanks, it wasn't pleasant to drink.

But when around noon, I opened the galley tap to rinse a plate, I noticed the water streaming out was tinted black. Alarmed, I crossed

over to the bilge, opened the hatch . . . and almost fell in! The water in it glinted darkly, its surface covered with a slick black metallic film. Diesel! If there was diesel in the bilge, there was a good chance it had seeped into the water tanks too. It wasn't hard to figure out what must have happened.

The water and diesel tanks lay side by side, under the floorboards on the starboard and port sides of the boat. They were separated by a hollow wall called a cofferdam to prevent the two liquids from mixing. Each tank was covered by a metal lid, bolted shut and sealed. But the rough and rumble of the sea must have damaged the seals, causing the diesel to leak out and contaminate the bilge and water tanks.

Let alone drink it, I couldn't even drain the polluted water into the ocean for fear of setting off a marine tragedy! My thoughts turned frantically to the water bottles. They were now my only source of drinking water. I quickly combed the boat to make an inventory of every full bottle I could find. I found few.

Several bottles had leaked dry and were now rolling around emptily on the floor of the bosun store, as useful to me as flotsam. Some appeared contaminated. I salvaged only ten bottles good enough to drink. Even if I drank one litre a day, the water wouldn't last until the end of the voyage, which was still a couple of weeks away!

I decided to scour the boat for any other fluids that might substitute for water. I rummaged in the stores and on the shelves of the galley, and after an hour, inventoried my haul:

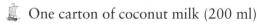 One carton of coconut milk (200 ml)

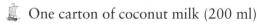 Four cans of energy drink (250 ml x 4)

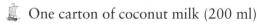 One packet of buttermilk that had turned halfway to yoghurt (useless)

This would hardly do. I had one last recourse left . . . to harvest the rain. It's far easier, thankfully, to harvest rain than to harvest a crop. While farmers can only reap what they sow, a harvester of rain can cup everything the heavens send. All that's needed are worthy vessels.

Thankfully, three days after I discovered the oil spill, the skies sent rain.

We were just north of Mauritius, about to enter the ITCZ, when clouds massed overhead. They gathered in low grey numbers like soldiers in iron armour, and at the signal of a thunderclap, rained vigorously down on us. I danced. And then, holding up my parched face to the cool water, I soaked it in.

Allowing the first few minutes of the shower to wash the salt and dirt off the air, the boat and me, I set to work. I rigged the waterproof Bimini, or sunshade, over the cockpit and planted a bucket alongside, ready to tip the water into it when the canvas filled up. This I then filtered through a square of cloth to sieve out any grit, and collected the relatively clean water into spare bottles.

The downpour lasted thirty minutes, and by the end of it, I was a wealthy man, with a rich harvest of ten litres of rainwater. Taken with the packaged water I had set aside, I now had nearly twice as much water as before!

# Water Harvesting at Sea

The heavens were in the mood to give because over the next couple of days, we were visited by more squalls, each refilling my water reserves . . . that is, all the empty bottles I could find!

What this also meant was I could now bathe more frequently!

So it was with a fresh suit of skin and a new surge of spirit that I prepared to cross the equator for the second and final time on the voyage.

*Mhadei* was too clever by half to pass the great ticker tape of the equator on a less than ordinary day. The clever thing chose 20 March, spring equinox, when day and night are finely balanced, to cross the line . . . for the seventh time in her life and the first time that year. Keeping with custom, I observed the same equatorial rituals as before. I made Lord Varuna an offering of popcorn and poured into his wide, watery mouth a capful of agave, a distilled spirit, to wash the kernels down.

I was inching home little by little, but there was no time to think about it. The days were hectic as ever as I went about my usual chores under the gaze of a glowering sun. The heat had started to close in and squeeze my brain like a pair of pincers. When I couldn't bear it, I'd duck into the cabin and stay out of the sun's reach for the length of the day, surfacing on deck for routine checks only when the star was well on its way west.

Sleep came in fits and starts, and as if measured by an egg timer, lasted but a few boiling minutes. But when it came, it brought dreams of such piercing lucidity and colour, I wasn't always sure which side up was reality, and which illusion . . .

The whale, however, insisted it was real.

The sun had set, the air had cooled and the water had turned a gunmetal grey, creased with dark lines like crumpled paper. Slowly a crease widened, opened like an envelope, and a head pushed out, arched and obsidian.

It wasn't looking at me, but in the general direction from which I had sailed. 'That's that,' it said in a low, gurgling voice, as if its mouth was full of water. Whether it spoke through its mouth or its blowhole I couldn't tell, but a spray of mist fountained at the same time.

'What do you mean, what's "that"?' I inquired, wiping the mist off my face.

'You're nearly home. You've circled the world, you proved that you could, and now the journey is coming to an end,' it answered. 'No more of here and forever . . . of this and that.'

I looked sadly at this and that—the sky and sea above and around me. Then I looked back at the whale. But it was gone. Without my noticing, without a goodbye, it had slipped back into the envelope, leaving a whale-sized hole in my heart.

By now, a spry north-westerly wind had picked us up and swept us across the sea towards the Maldives. The 1200 islands and sandbanks that make up this island-nation arc upwards towards the Lakshadweep Islands like a trail of breadcrumbs leading up to that loaf of land called India.

About 270 nautical miles south of the Maldives, I passed the atolls of the Chagos Archipelago. As I entered the neighbourhood of the islands, an image lit up in my mind, clear and bright, as if only just caught by

the spotlight of my eye. But it had been burnt into my memory from another, older journey.

Back then . . .

Night had fallen and the sea was a bed of resting ravens, bobbing black. The moon was nowhere in the sky. Suddenly, as if by some spectral force, the dark waters around us lit up like an electric blanket. A ghostly blueish-green light rippled in tiny pinpricks across the water's surface, covering a patch of the sea as wide as a wheat field. It was like sailing through an LED dream.

They were bioluminescent plankton, the floating food of the ocean. These microscopic organisms emit a cold light when disturbed or in defence, creating a phantasmagoric phenomenon on the sea. Charles Darwin saw it. Joshua Slocum saw it too and wrote: 'The sea, where the sloop disturbed it, seemed all ablaze so that by its light I could see the smallest articles on deck, and her wake was a path of fire.'

Hoping to catch the lights this time around too, I kept a close vigil on the waters. But nothing, not even an electric eel, flipped a switch.

By the third week of March, I reached the Maldives.

This 'garland of islands'—which is what 'Maldives' means, from the Sanskrit word *maladvipa*—once supplied parts of the world with loose change in the form of cowrie shells. In those times of motley currency, the Moroccan traveller Ibn Batuta, from the early 1300s, wrote that the Maldivians traded their little white mollusc shells for a wide assortment of goods, including Bengal rice, since the crop wouldn't grow on the low-lying islands. (They're one of the lowest-lying islands in the world, and the slightest increase in sea level can sink them.)

As I cut past these islands, I had to negotiate the paralysing doldrums that had held us captive for a whole week on our way out of the northern hemisphere, in November 2012. Dreading similar detention,

I knew I had to find a quick exit through the windless passage. Being stuck there once again was not a risk I was willing to take, not least because I was still anxious about my fraught water reserves.

To my relief, satellite imagery revealed a narrow, fleeting corridor of wind slicing right through the doldrums, like Moses's dry walkway through the Red Sea. All I had to do now was find my way into that wind tunnel.

Thankfully, my luck had held out this far, and had no intention of leaving just yet. It did not take long to find my way into the corridor and with this rare wind in my back, I made it out of the doldrums in twelve swift, short hours.

~~~

Of all the colours that had leached out of my memory from my long days on the ocean, I only mourned the loss of green—the colour of the paddy fields of Kuttanad, the rubber trees of Nedumkunnam, the coconut stands along the Mandovi and the knitted rain trees of Colaba. After 150 days on the water, my eyes had become accustomed to an unaltering band of blues, greys and blacks. Imagine, then, my surprise when a bright emerald crop sprung up in the closed air of the cabin.

The onions had sprouted! What remained of the few bulbs I had packed at the start of the journey had sent up shoots in the moist sea air! Their long, green blades stuck out messily from the corded sling like an aeroponics experiment gone frightfully right!

Other signs of land-life appeared on the boat. I'd sailed up to the 10th parallel north, the latitude level with Nedumkunnam, my grandfather's village in Kerala, when without warning dragonflies swarmed in. I later learnt they may have been the forerunners of the annual dragonfly migration across the Western Indian Ocean. Millions of them glide from East Africa to India, riding the currents of the southwest monsoon winds that spring up around May. In October, another generation is ferried back to Africa, this time on the wings of the northeast monsoons. This travelling species is called the globe skimmer or wandering glider, and I believe they'd stopped by the boat to say hello, one wanderer to another.

Their webbed wings netting rainbows where they caught the light, the dragonflies spread across the sails, bunks and navigation table, casting tiny kaleidoscopes around the cabin. The last four months at sea had felt like a lifetime, and I could now no longer decide if home was behind me or before me. So I simply decided to follow the dragonflies, whose arrowed bodies pointed the way.

# Closing the Loop

Somewhere in the first century AD (the exact date is unknown), a sailor from Alexandria (whose name is unknown), wrote a handy navigational guide to the Western Indian Ocean, a kind of sailing instruction manual. Just like a modern GPS that gives directions to a place and says where to stop for a burger, the *Periplus of the Erythrean Sea* did something similar 2000 years ago.

It offered sailors detailed instructions about the harbours and seaports rimming the coasts, telling them what stars to follow and which winds to harness to get there. It warned them about the mood of different currents and showed them how to tell if land was near. 'The sea will change colour and you might even see serpents,' it helpfully said. 'The snakes are large and black around the Gulf of Khambhat in Gujarat, and smaller and green or gold further down India's west coast.'

If the sea changed colour or snakes broke the surface I couldn't say, because on the evening of 31 March, my eyes were nowhere near the water. They were fixed like two sharp tacks on distant land. Hidden at first in a swirl of grey mist and smoke, like a mountain behind a cloud, its lines grew bigger and bolder as I approached. The haze that wrapped around it like a boa gradually loosened its grip . . . and suddenly, as if from out of nowhere, there lay the city that launched a thousand ships—Mumbai!

I was back.

I had closed the loop. Knotted the bow. Girdled the globe. Circled the earth.

### *And completed Sagar Parikrama II!*

It was 4 p.m. when *Mhadei* and I drew up outside Mumbai Harbour. The sun was inches from the horizon and the sea was shimmering gold. After the acres of empty oceans I had crossed, the small harbour seemed a hive, thrumming with action. A cruise ship filled to the brim with tourists crossed me on one side, and small yachts and fishing vessels bobbed idly about on the other. It felt strange and stifling to be suddenly surrounded like this.

Now although I had reached the gateposts, I couldn't yet enter the city because the navy had asked me to stall and stay out of sight. (As much as it was possible to stay hidden just outside one of the busiest cities in the world. Or maybe, that's what made camouflage possible). I was instructed to enter the harbour only after dark to keep my arrival secret from the public. For the time being.

So I waited obediently in the cockpit, biding my time, a very different man from the one who had set out five months ago. My beard and hair had grown long and frizzy from the humidity at sea, my skin had turned to toast, my palms were calloused and hard as boards and a new crop of fine lines crowded the corners of my eyes from all that squinting in the sun.

Before I could take further stock of my weathering, I heard the rapid-fire of whirring blades. It was a naval helicopter, and from its cockpit, I could see a camera blinking rapidly as it shot picture after picture of the boat and me. The weight of the moment, however, was like a feather on my back, light and slight. It would only be much later when the hours stacked up and the congratulations poured in that the fact would sink like a lead line to the ocean floor . . .

I was the **first** Indian to circumnavigate the globe non-stop and unassisted.

The **second** Asian.

The **seventy-ninth** person in the world.

When I'd sailed out of Mumbai 150 days and seven hours ago, it was not for a trophy or a world record. I only wanted a Grand Adventure . . . an experience of intergalactic proportions! I wanted to hear what the great sailors had heard when they put their ear to the heart of the sea. But more than anything else, I wanted to know if I had what it took . . . the nerves and courage to sail alone around the world.

Turns out, I had.

~~~

At the appointed hour, I quietly crept into the harbour. Night had fallen by the time I crossed the buildings that were part of the navy's sea-facing offices. Before long, I passed my own waterfront office on Pilot Bunder Road. To know that in a matter of days I'd once again be boxed in and pinned to a desk made my hair curl even further. Not even the worst Force 10 storm on the entire expedition had struck such dread in my heart. I quickly turned my back on the thought. No point extending an early welcome to a bad feeling.

In the distance, the Gateway of India loomed like the massive cardboard cut-out it once was. At the pier below, ferryboats massed like mussels, their railings threaded with colourful winking lights that lit up the last of the day's tourists swaying on their decks.

Entering the harbour at night was like walking barefoot into a dark tool shed. Fishing nets and flotsam floated about invisibly, and to run into them would be like stepping on an upturned nail. Just as I had done when sailing out of the harbour, I had to keep a close watch on the sea to make sure the path was clear going back in.

Suddenly, a couple of bright lights tunnelled through the darkness and moved steadily in my direction. An inflatable boat. And within it a sight I hadn't encountered in over a hundred days. Friends. The faces of Captain Donde, Ratnakar, my assistant Alam and half a dozen colleagues from the naval office loomed into view, crowding the night air with wild cheers, whistles, claps and hoots—a clamour loud enough to raise the bones of the fish on the seabed.

'Good to see you, Abhilash!'

'You did it, man!'

'How does it feel to be home?'

'You've lost weight!'

Amid all that excitement and hubbub, a box of popcorn and a can of cola were passed up to me. Captain Donde and Alam climbed aboard my boat and hugged me. Wasting no time, both boats headed into the floodlit Naval Dockyard and moored in the considerable shadow of the hulking grey warship, the INS *Delhi*. It was the very vessel I was stationed on as Captain Donde's shore support!

As we docked and I prepared to step off my boat, something hit me like a 10-ton anchor. Since setting foot on her deck at the start of the expedition five months ago, this was the very first time I was about to leave *Mhadei*. My heart cracked.

*Mhadei*, my companion and friend, had travelled the world with me on this adventure of a lifetime. And now the adventure had ended and we were parting ways. Although I knew I could see her anytime I wanted at the naval dockyard in Goa, to which she would eventually return, I also knew this was our last great escapade together. However, I consoled myself with the thought that it wasn't goodbye yet, for we still had the celebratory reception to attend in a few days.

I climbed down the yacht and up the ladder of the warship. On the deck, I was seized by a crowd slightly bigger than the welcome party in the harbour. My arrival was still a secret, even to those in the navy, and only a select few had gathered to welcome me home. Among them were all the admirals and senior officers of the navy's Western Command.

The first celebration—and there were many to follow—was a simple, but by no means quiet, affair. A bottle of champagne was popped and popcorn was piled up in buckets, enough to feed a whole movie hall! And everywhere and all the while, questions and congratulations flew like sea spray. I was hugged and thumped on the back so many times, I would have keeled over were it not for the two uniformed sailors propping me up on either side.

The pair had been assigned to me not because I was suddenly important, but because I was horribly unsteady! Accustomed to the constant motion of the boat, my sea legs needed time to adjust to land. They wobbled uncertainly when I stood, and it was with great effort that I managed to stay upright.

They did, however, snap to attention when the commander-in-chief of the Western Naval Command strode up. Vice Admiral Shekhar Sinha was the one to gift me the binoculars at the Gateway of India 150 days ago. He now gripped my hand and said in a voice trimmed with pride, 'You have turned geography into history. Very warm congratulations young man!'

If the reception had been a hushed affair—without the jostle of reporters or the flare of firecrackers—it was only because it was not yet time to announce my arrival. That day was around the corner, and it was to be a million times grander than my send-off. But I didn't know it yet.

After the official welcome drew to a close at around 10.30 p.m., a few of us friends headed back to *Mhadei* for a second party, taking along pizzas generously provided by the cooks on the INS *Delhi*. While I hadn't lost my tongue, it had become stiff after months of neglect, and I found it difficult to contribute to the torrent of chatter. My friends thankfully did most of the talking, catching me up on all that had happened while I was away . . . which, turns out, wasn't very much after all! I'd travelled all the way around the earth and returned to find things exactly as I'd left them.

Finally, at around one in the morning, we decided to call it a night. For the second time, I said goodbye to the boat and stepped on to the pier and into a waiting car that would drive me to the mess. This was the naval officers' dining and living quarters in Colaba, where I had a room. *Mhadei* would remain at the dockyard for the rest of the week until it was time to step on stage.

The car sped down the yellow streets of night-time Mumbai, quiet and still like the doldrums. As I cut through the city, hemmed in by tall walls and pinned down by row upon row of cars and motorbikes, the open fields of the sea had already started to take on the smoky aspect of a recent dream. *Was I really there? Were the storms for real?* I wondered for a second. Then I furled and unfurled my hands and felt the skin crack around the cuts and callouses made by the salt and the sheets.

I had sailed all right.

That night as I lay in a bed that did not roll, in a room that did not rattle, I grew seasick . . . sick for the sea. It was 1 April. Fool's Day. The words of Bernard Moitessier came back to me. 'There are two terrible things for a man: not to have fulfilled his dream, and to have fulfilled it.'

I knew what he meant. What was left to do now? What greater challenge could I take up? Wasn't a solo circumnavigation the ultimate challenge?

'Not when you can make it a race,' I heard Bernard say. I grinned in the dark. The Golden Globe Race. That would be next. Not just a sail alone around the world, but an all-out sprint, going head-to-head with a dozen of the best sailors on the planet. I wasn't ready to drop anchor just yet.

Only then did I fall off to sleep, with my head full of the sea.

# Finding My Land Legs

The first phone call I made when I checked into the mess was to my parents in Kochi. I had last spoken to them at Cape Horn.

'Remember what I said? Nothing would harm you,' began my mother, her voice cracking, but in a good way. We chatted for a while about my journey and our family, and then they broke the news to me . . .

'Your grandfather Philip is dying,' said my father.

My stomach turned.

Philip was my favourite grandparent. I remembered all the holidays I had spent with him, learning how to fish, slice a jackfruit, milk the cows. Grown-ups often tell you what to do, but Grandpa Philip *showed* me . . . how to work hard, be independent and use every skill I had, because that's exactly what he did. He had a big role to play in the person I had become and the things I had achieved.

'I'll come down to visit him as soon as the reception is over,' I promised.

~~~

Now, although we had arrived on 31 March, it was a whole week later that an official reception was to be staged for *Mhadei* and me. The navy had organized a great big celebration, to be attended by none other than the President of the country himself, Mr Pranab Mukherjee! The President was also the commander-in-chief of the Indian Armed Forces, so they couldn't have chosen a more fitting guest of honour. But being a busy man, Mr Mukherjee would only be available to receive me on 6 April. Until then, I had to lay low. News of my arrival was held back from the public to keep the welcome fresh and exciting. What I was instructed to do in the meanwhile was stay in my room and speak to no one. Not a problem. I was used to that!

It wasn't the 'speak-to-no-one' bit that was hard to do, but the 'go-nowhere' order.

After nearly one-third of a year on the open ocean, to be cooped up for even an hour in a tiny room was like stuffing a whale into a matchbox. But I did as I was told. I lay on my bed, and with glazed eyes watched the hours mount one above the other like sheep forming an animal pyramid.

Luckily, an important matter did require me to step out of the mess and into the city. I had to go to the passport office at Yellow Gate in the Fort area, not far from my office, to get my passport stamped. As I stepped into the taxi that would take me there, I hoped I wouldn't have a hard time of it this time, like I had the last.

This is how it went before . . .

'You are leaving the country, yes?' the passport officer prompted.

'Yes,' I replied.

'And the date you are leaving is 1 November?'

'Yes.'

'And to which country are you headed?'

'None.'

(I was starting to enjoy this.)

'But you're leaving India?'

'Yes.'

'On a boat?'

'Yes.'

'And you're not going to dock at any country?'

'No.'

(This could go on and on. I wasn't enjoying it anymore.)

Urgent intervention was needed. I requested Captain Donde to come down to the office and explain the mission to the officer, who perhaps thought I was pulling a prank on him. Not that I could blame him. No one had ever come to an Indian passport office with such an absurd request before. Captain Donde had made four halts during his circumnavigation, so the officer he'd met had no reason to doubt him.

Finally, after much eyebrow-arching, the officer was convinced. He reached for my passport, took his important rubber stamp and pressed down on the page, only to stamp it upside down in his confusion.

Five months later, I was back in the same office, hoping to meet the same officer and see the look on his face. 'I wonder what he'll say this time.' I chuckled.

To my bad luck, it was someone else at the counter. He, however, had read about the mission in the newspapers, and without a moment's hesitation imprinted the necessary stamp of admission. The right side up.

After the passport office, I returned to my room to be holed up for another couple of days. My only visitors were Admiral Awati and Captain Donde. I have never been much of a talker, much less a 'small talker'. But having had no company for so long, I now found it doubly difficult to fill my conversations with the little things people say to plug the gaps between one subject and the next. I had lost the caulking, the stuff between the boat's seams that keeps the water out, and now my conversations were flooded with little silences.

Once again, I resumed my solitary vigil, waiting for the day I could finally go free. I took my meals in my room, eating whatever was cooked in the mess kitchen. There was nothing I particularly craved, although some popcorn would have helped pass the hours.

Midway through the week, I stepped out once again. Hailing a taxi, I headed to an electronics shop midtown to buy a few parts for my new laptop. Sitting in the back of the cab, I watched people and places flit by as if on a giant screen in a cinema hall. I can't say I was enjoying it very much. The car horns, billboards, shouts and smoke were overwhelming, a maelstrom that was more unnerving than the real thing at sea.

The taxi halted at a traffic signal and suddenly a head poked in through the window.

'Can I have change for Rs 50, please? I need a tenner.' A man getting out of another cab needed a smaller note to pay his fare.

I was startled. It was as if while watching the city as a movie, one of the actors had suddenly stepped out of the screen.

I fished out a ten-rupee note from my pocket and handed it to him without a word. 'Keep it.' I gestured vaguely.

*What should I have said?* I asked myself after the man had left.

*Here you go?*

*Why not?*

*Happy to help?*

*Do you need more?*